BEGINNER'S GUIDE

HOUSE PLANT CARE MADE EASY

Your go-to resource to help you choose plants, optimize plant health, grow with confidence and create beautiful indoor spaces

Nydia Needham

Copyright © 2024 .

All rights reserved. No part of this book may be reproduced, stored, or transmitted by any means—whether auditory, graphic, mechanical, or electronic—without written permission of both publisher and author, except in the case of brief excerpts used in critical articles and reviews. Unauthorized reproduction of any part of this work is illegal and is punishable by law.

978-1-915217-41-7 (paperback)

CONTENTS

Introduction vii

STEP 1: PLANT SELECTION AND CONSIDERATIONS

Chapter 1: Which Plants are Right for You?... 3
Chapter 2: Key considerations: light, humidity, design & layout 14

STEP 2: DAY-TO-DAY PLANT CARE ROUTINES

Chapter 3: Basic Plant Care & Maintenance 35
Chapter 4: Regular Plant Maintenance (Daily/Weekly)......................... 52
Chapter 5: Regular Plant Maintenance (Monthly/Yearly).................... 63
Chapter 6: The Toughest Plants Around 71

STEP 3: TROUBLESHOOTING AND EXPANDING

Chapter 7: Common Plant Problems 79
Chapter 8: Propagation and Potting.. 98
Chapter 9: Automation and Artificial Lighting................................... 110
Chapter 10: Taking It to the Next Level.. 120

Conclusion 129
Appendix – Pests and Disease... 133
References 139
Houseplant Directory.. 141

Scan the QR code below to get your FREE Houseplant Directory!

INTRODUCTION

When I first got my own place, I went and bought four houseplants from the local garden center. They looked nice and healthy and green, they had easy names like 'cheese plant' and 'spider plant' and 'rubber plant,' they were already in pretty pots ready to put on the windowsill; how much trouble could they be?

Well, I killed them all.

First of all I forgot to water them. I was kinda busy, and I just forgot. One of them started sulking. Its leaves turned brown. It died.

So I thought 'Okay, plants want water, my bad; let's make sure you all get some water.' Noah's flood had nothing on what I gave those plants over the next week. And then one of them just keeled over and died. Turned out the stem was rotten all the way through.

Two gone, two left. A neighbor told me they wanted more light so I should put them in the yard for a while. That seemed to work for a while, but then the weather forecaster announced a cold snap, so I brought them in and parked them on the kitchen countertop for the night.

The next morning, I came down to find slugs and snails crawling all over the counter. They'd come in with the houseplants. Horrible! (It could have been worse. A friend living in Arizona managed to bring a baby rattlesnake in with her lemon tree!).

So the plants went out again til I had time to get my kitchen de-slugged and check the pots, and then there was a cold snap the next night too, and that was the end for plant number three.

Plant four, on the other hand, seemed almost invincible. It grew and grew and grew, and even produced little baby plants… and then it died. When I chucked it out in the trash, I saw the whole pot was full of roots. It seemed there was no earth left at all, just roots. Now, I know that's called 'pot-bound.' Then, I just thought it was weird.

Maybe you've had a similar experience. Or maybe one of your friends managed to run through a lot of houseplants in a short while. That might put you off houseplants for life!

Or maybe, like a lot of people, you just worry that houseplants aren't for you, or that you're not the kind of person who can look after them successfully. You might be anxious that:

- You don't have enough time.
- You don't have enough space.
- You have a 'black thumb.'
- All houseplants are crazily high-maintenance.
- You lack experience at looking after houseplants.
- You lack the expertise that's necessary.
- You killed a plant once and you worry you'll do it again.

You're not alone. I can sympathize with all of them. I understand your pain!

After my mass plant-murder experience, I didn't touch houseplants for ages. I became a keen gardener, started learning about plants and permaculture, and even planted fruit trees, but the only way plants came in the house was if I was going to eat them. But finally, I brought a lovely little pelargonium in for the winter, and the lemony smell of its leaves made my house fragrant and welcoming, and, somehow, it never left. Now it's been joined by other plants and my gardening knowledge has helped me keep them all happy and thriving.

So I'm here to tell you that most houseplants aren't that difficult to keep happy. There is no secret knowledge you need, and no 'green thumb' that you lack. This book will talk you through the basics of houseplant care, beginning with choosing the right plants. If you're a beginner, don't choose a tropical plant that needs high temperature and high humidity and special fertilizers; choose a nice, easy plant that won't make too many demands.

I've used my own experience to find shortcuts and smart solutions to common problems. I've learned how to assess a plant's health quickly and work out what it needs from me. I've learned how to organize chores like watering and fertilizing so they take minimal time, and I've learned what tricks work and which ones don't. I've even found out how to reduce my costs by getting my plants to produce new ones for me, and how to manage one or two of the more difficult species.

I had to learn by trial and error. I found plenty of information for free on the internet, but some of it was contradictory, some of it was way too technical to be useful, and some of it was just plain wrong. I found a couple of books, but I think they were written for people my grandad's age who wanted to win prizes for their exhibition orchids, and who had tropical glasshouses with irrigation systems, not for people who just wanted some nice plants in their apartment (I still found a few little nuggets of information in them, though).

I've written this book to try to save you the trial and error (it might also save you a bit of money on dead plants and expensive gadgets). I hope it will give you the confidence and knowledge you need to fill your house full of wonderful houseplants and flowers. They'll give your home a feeling of life and freshness that you can't get any other way.

Let's get started!

STEP 1

PLANT SELECTION AND CONSIDERATIONS

CHAPTER 1

WHICH PLANTS ARE RIGHT FOR YOU?

One of my friends fell in love with an orchid. It was a fantastic flower, bright purple patterned with bright white dots and streaks. I can understand why she loved it. She bought the plant from an online seller, and she was aghast when it arrived, a scruffy, struggling little plant in a plastic pot. Was this the beautiful orchid she'd fallen in love with?

She repotted it, she fed it, she watered it, she put it in the sun. But it didn't want to grow. It struggled for a couple of years, but it never flowered. And then it died.

She found out later that it was considered one of the most difficult orchids to grow, and orchids are notorious as one of the most difficult plants. They need specific varieties of potting mix. They're highly intolerant of over-watering but they need high levels of humidity in the air. They need plenty of light but they don't like direct sunlight, which can burn their leaves. In a word, most orchids are *picky*.

This is a common mistake for all kinds of plant lovers – buying plants that are too demanding, or that don't suit the conditions of their particular house or garden. Are you buying from catalogue pictures instead of reading up on the plant's particular needs? Are you buying because you saw a 'top ten houseplants' list on *The Spruce*, rather than thinking what plant would look best (and grow well) in your kitchen? Or are you just buying what was in the supermarket's garden aisle, on impulse?

So let's take a step back and think about some basics that can help you avoid this mistake. First of all, why do you want houseplants in the first place?

There are all kinds of benefits to having houseplants. One is that they can reduce air pollution, particularly from VOCs (volatile organic compounds) that are found in common household products and often in building materials like paints. That can help prevent respiratory ailments. However, you'll need enough plants – say fifteen or eighteen reasonably sized plants for a family home[1].

Some houseplants are also believed to relieve allergies by filtering allergens out of the air. There should be less dust and less mold if your houseplants are thriving.

And there's also a benefit that comes from feeling close to nature. Just as a walk in the forest makes you feel happy and at peace, watering your pot plants can become an exercise in contentment. There's even a microorganism in potting soil that can help trigger the release of the 'happy chemical' serotonin in your body.

And of course if you grow flowering plants, there's nothing like the fragrance and color of flowers for improving your day. Although we buy flowers for someone in hospital mainly because it's a social gesture, in fact quite a few studies[2] have shown that patients with flowers in the room, or with a view over a garden or woodlands, tend to recover more quickly.

Plants absorb carbon dioxide and release oxygen, making your bedroom a healthier place while you're asleep by adding oxygen to the air. This might be one reason studies such as K.T. Han's 2009 experiment in Taiwan[3] have shown that plants in the classroom can help students concentrate better (that effect works in offices, too).

In a dry interior, having a good assortment of houseplants could help to increase the humidity. However, make sure your plants can cope with the dryness; if central heating turns your apartment into a desert, don't buy orchids or ferns!

Finally, some of the plants you might want to grow indoors are edible and medicinal plants, which are often expensive or difficult to buy elsewhere. For instance, you might want an aloe vera plant for its sap, which can help treat burns and other skin irritations. Or you might want basil, cilantro, and chives for your kitchen. You might even fancy growing a citrus tree, though you may have to wait a long time for your fruit.

Your specific reasons for wanting houseplants could affect which plants you choose. For instance, if you are worried about Sick Building Syndrome (Sick Building Syndrome is a condition in which people develop health conditions as

---

[1] NASA clean air study
[2] S.H. Park, R.H. Mattoson - Therapeutic influences of plants in hospital rooms on surgical recovery HortScience, 44 (2009), pp. 102-105

[3] Han, K. T., (2009). Influence of limitedly visible leafy indoor plants on the psychology, behavior, and health of students at a junior high school in Taiwan. Environment and Behavior, 41(5), 658-692.

a result of living or working in a particular building) some of the plants you could consider are the following:

- **Spider plants** (Chlorophytum comosum), which are very easy to care for, are self-propagating, and non-toxic; these help to eliminate formaldehyde and xylene from the air.

- **Dracaenas,** which are also easy to grow, and help to eliminate toluene, benzene, trichloroethylene (however, they are toxic to pets).

- **Mum** (Chrysanthemum), which is easy to grow, but only purifies the air when it's flowering (and is also toxic).

- **Bamboo palms** (Chamaedora seifrizii) can help to keep the air humid as well as helping to eliminate lots of VOCs, and are safe for your pets.

- **Rubber plant** (Ficus elastica) is easy to grow but toxic to pets.

- **Devil's ivy** (Golden pothos) is almost impossible to kill and is a really effective air purifier, but again, is not safe for pets.

- **Areca palm** (Chrysalidocarpus lutescens) is a thirsty plant which is pretty easy to grow, it's non-toxic and it eliminates a whole load of chemicals from the air.

And of course, if plants are toxic to your animal companions, you won't want them around should you have small children, either. Still, there are enough safe plants on the list for you to purify the air and beautify your home without any anxiety.

If you're interested in plants you can eat, the easiest way to start might be the way many children do, growing mustard and cress on the windowsill. You might want herbs in the kitchen – basil, chives, parsley, cilantro, mint (indestructible!), rosemary, sage, thyme or oregano. Some vegetables can be regrown from scraps, such as celery and green onions; you can just grow those in water, no soil needed. You might also want to grow microgreens like arugula, lettuce, and baby spinach.

You could go further. Potatoes are actually quite easy (if potentially a bit messy) to grow indoors; the most difficult part is getting a big enough pot or bag to grow them in. And if you have a lot of light, you could try bell peppers, chillis and tomatoes, or even bananas (you may not get fruit but a banana tree is a beautiful plant, anyway). Or you could try growing mushrooms – you can buy windowsill kits to grow shitake or oyster mushrooms, which are really easy to cultivate and ideal for beginners.

If, on the other hand, you want houseplants to make your home more beautiful, then you will probably prefer ferns, palms, snake plant (Sansevieria), and plants like Alocasia with huge, sometimes variegated, leaves. You might want to invest in one or two larger plants, like a monstera or rubber plant, and add trailing plants like spider plant for hanging pots, or trailing down from a high shelf.

You might also want natural fragrance in your home. This would give you some interesting options, such as Arabian jasmine, citrus trees with their scented flowers, Cuban oregano (Plectranthus amboinicus) with its spikier scent, or even orchids like Sharry Baby Sweet Fragrance, which smells of chocolate! Orange jessamine is a nice, tight bush with glossy green foliage, which emits a lovely orangey fragrance when it blooms. Or you could grow scented geraniums (technically, pelargoniums), which are tolerant and easy to propagate, and come in lemon-, ginger-, nutmeg- and even chocolate-scented varieties.

If your main motivation is the sense of well-being you'll get from having plants growing in your home, you can choose from any of the plants mentioned in this book. Choose plants that make you feel happy when you look at them or smell them, or that remind you of happy times (plants your grandmother grew, for instance).

You have needs, or wishes, that your houseplants will fulfill. But you also need to think about what the plants need, and whether your home can provide it.

Although you might think that if you're keeping plants indoors, your geographical location doesn't matter, that's not actually the case. True, your house is always going to be warm, so you don't have to worry about outside temperatures in winter. But plants have other requirements, particularly hours of sunlight and intensity of light. You may need to move plants to a south-facing windowsill in winter if they aren't getting enough light; on the other hand, if you have a bright summer, some of your plants may find the light too strong, and you'll have to move them to a more sheltered area.

Of course, if you are really set on keeping plants that need brighter, or more, light than you can give them, you might consider using artificial light. All kinds of grow-lights are now available, and just a couple of supplementary hours in winter can make a big difference.

Many popular houseplants are tropical and need high temperatures of around 65-75F during the day (18-24C). Below 50F they may sulk. But higher temperatures indoors can also be a problem, since indoor plants don't get the humidity or cool breezes they would if they were outside; they wilt, and they stop breathing, which means you won't get the air purification benefits you would otherwise.

While they'll need some ventilation, most houseplants don't like being near a draft; and while they need warmth, they probably don't want to sit right on top of a radiator.

As well as being relatively warm, our homes are often quite dry, particularly in winter when the central heating is on. Central heating can really dry out the air, and those houseplants which like humidity around 40-50% (like ferns and orchids) won't enjoy 5-10% humidity. There are a few ways to help them out, though, like putting them in the bathroom.

You want to think about your space before buying plants. Do you have enough room for a really big houseplant? Or only a couple of windowsills? How hot do you keep your home? Do you have particular bright spots that catch the sun?

You might also want to do some hard thinking about where these plants come from and the impact of houseplant demand on wildlife. Some plants have become extremely rare in the wild owing to the activities of illegal harvesters. On the other hand, growing houseplants can preserve rare species, such as rare cacti that are threatened by habitat loss. Make sure you buy from reputable sellers, who propagate their own plants and don't buy illegally traded plants.

It's also worth thinking about the fact that most houseplants aren't indigenous, if you live in a temperate climate. There's always a danger of non-native plants escaping; in Florida, for example, 'escaped' asparagus fern, English ivy, snake plant, and wild taro (Colocasia) have become a big problem. So be careful if you're disposing of a plant you don't like!

WHAT TYPE OF PLANTS DO YOU LIKE?

My grandmother loved dark, glossy leaves. She lived in a rather gloomy house and her choice of houseplant just made it worse. As a result, I grew up liking vivid colors in houseplants, and I prefer ferns and bamboos to snake plants or rubber plants. A friend of mine just loves cacti, and waits eagerly for them to flower; I'm always careful about just where I sit when I visit her apartment!

Everyone has their own taste in houseplants, so don't worry if *World of Interiors* is telling you that you 'ought' to have a particular plant; if you don't like it, don't get it! Before you buy houseplants, it's good to think through plants or gardens you've particularly admired in the past.

Maybe you love the tropical beauties? Orchids are one possibility, or strelitzia with its wonderful single flower; or you might try brightly colored bromeliads. For a home jungle, mix your flowering plants with plenty of big leaves like elephant's ear, kentia palm, weeping fig, or monstera.

Succulents might be more to your taste. These plants have adapted to dry climates by storing their water in their stems and leaves. Some, like the snake plant, can make good accent plants; aloe and jade plant are easy to grow, and impressive. A good accent plant will attract the eye and provide a focal point for a room. Or you could fill pots with an assortment of different cactus species, such as crassula, aeonium, or houseleek.

You might prefer delicate plants like ferns and tree ferns. However, they love humidity, so they are not the easiest plants to grow (outside the bathroom). Boston fern, rabbit's foot and birds nest are probably the easiest to start with, working up to the magnificent Stag Horn fern.

For a 'cottage garden' feel, you could choose European plants like mint, tulips, snowdrops, English ivy, and cyclamen. Most of these could even go out on the balcony or in the garden over the summer.

You might also want to think about your personality as a houseplant owner. Are you a nurturer, who really wants to get involved? Then you could enjoy looking after ferns, alocasia, papyrus, fiddle leaf fig, bonsai, orchids, stromanthe, or maranta. Or are you a distant parent, who wants plants that will look after themselves? Then cacti and succulents are your go-to plants, plus maybe some yucca, or a ponytail palm, and snake plants.

The tables below show some plants to choose from. The first table shows the ease of caring for specific plants; I'd encourage you to look at the low-maintenance ones while you're getting started. The next table looks at particular categories you might be interested in, such as plants with colorful flowers, or plants that can cope with low light levels.

Picking your house plants by ease of care		
Low maintenance	**A little care**	**Demanding**
Cacti	Easier orchids	Most ferns
Succulents	Begonia	Bonsai trees
Snake plant	Corn plant	Papyrus
Yucca	Peace lily	Air plants
Wax plant	Giant taro	Stromanthe
Spurge	Bromeliads	
ZZ or Zanzibar plant	Zebra plant	
Marimo moss balls	Prayer plant	
Ponytail palm		
Spider plant		
Wandering Jew		
Swiss cheese plant		
Philodendron		
Asparagus fern		

Picking your houseplants by category			
Type of plant	Example plants		
Flowering	Wax begonia Orchids Christmas cactus Flaming Katy Geranium Madagascar jasmine	Bromeliads Pink anthurium African violet Amaryllis Peace lily Wax plant	Cyclamen Hyacinth Tulip Daffodil Bougainvillea
Colorful foliage	Nerve plant Aluminium plant Chinese evergreen Anthurium Doc Block F2	Rex begonia Triostar stromanthe Purple velvet plant Philodendron mican	Ti plant Purple shamrock Anthurium King of Spades
Low-light	Spider plant Peperomia Staghorn fern Philodendron Swiss cheese plant Wax Begonia Guzmania Nerve plant	Maidenhair fern Lucky bamboo English ivy Flamingo flower Chinese evergreen Arrowhead vine Maranta Polka dot plant	Snake plant Cast iron plant ZZ plant Dragon tree Corn plant Wax plant Parlor palm
Air purifiers	Corn plant English Ivy Snake plant Kentia palm	Rubber plant Aloe vera Chinese evergreen Pothos	Bamboo palm Spider plant Peace lily ZZ plant
Trailing plants	Pothos Heart-leaf Philodendron Lipstick plant Coral cactus Wax plant Tradescantia	Orchid cactus Staghorn fern String of pearls Burro's tail Spider plant	Red herringbone plant Fishbone cactus Chain cactus String of hearts Peperomia prostrata

Picking your houseplants by category			
Type of plant	Example plants		
Small plants	Croton petra Polka dot plant Houseleek Air plant Wax agave Flaming Katy	Pothos Chinese money plant Jade plant Lucky bamboo Lithops	Ponytail palm Christmas cactus String of pearls Asparagus fern Baby toes
Large plants	Money tree Rubber plant African fig tree Banyan fig Dumb cane	Swiss cheese plant Areca palm Kentia palm Bird of paradise Banana plant	Dragon tree Fiddle-leaf fig Yucca Elephant's ear Majesty palm
Succulents	Horse's teeth Fairy washboard Wax agave Common houseleek Living stone Pig's ear Panda plant	Agave Corsican stonecrop Burro's tail Moonstone Knoppies Gasteria Snake plant	Aeonium Gollum Jade Jade necklace vine Crassula Buddha's Temple Lace aloe Mother of pearl
Cacti	Angel wings cactus African milk tree Saguaro cactus Melon cactus	Nippel cactus Old lady cactus Powder puff cactus Star cactus	Christmas cactus Barrel cactus Rat tail cactus Moon cactus

SOME COMMON HOUSEPLANT MYTHS

There are quite a lot of myths about keeping houseplants, and some of them may have made you reluctant to keep them, or less than confident about your ability to look after them. So let's just debunk a few of the fairy stories before getting on to the serious business of choosing your plants.

PONYTAIL PALM   RED HERRINGBONE

COMMON HOUSEPLANT MYTHS

- **Myth: You need a 'green thumb.'** While it's true that some people seem to have more luck with houseplants than others, that's usually because they have more knowledge about plants and perhaps a little bit more organization. It's nothing to do with green thumbs.
- **Myth: Houseplants need constant watering.** You know that's not true – cacti living in their natural environment sometimes go without water for over a year! In fact, overwatering is a really common way to kill off houseplants. Being away for a week is much less likely to hurt them!
- **Myth: Houseplants are poisonous to kids and pets.** There certainly are a number of plants which are toxic, but there is such a wide range of houseplants available that you can select safer choices if you wish. In fact, you might want to grow indoor cat grass for your feline companion!
- **Myth: You need to establish a strict watering schedule and stick to it.** That sounds like hard work, right? In fact, you don't generally need a strict schedule; for most plants just stick your finger in the soil in the pot to find out whether your plant needs a drink. If it's dried out, water it; if it hasn't, don't (note, there are some that are a little more fussy).
- **Myth: Indoor plants need lots of sunlight.** This is why most people automatically put plants on the windowsill. However, some houseplants prefer less sun, or want the light filtered so they don't burn. Always check what your plant likes before deciding where to put it.
- **Myth: You need to mist your plants regularly to keep up humidity.** While this is true for some plants, for most, you really don't need to go around with a spray bottle; most houseplants can cope with dryer air. If your house is dryer than normal, why don't you just grow succulents or cacti, which will enjoy the dryness?
- **Myth: Plants grow bigger if you put them in a bigger pot.** In fact, they're more likely to do well if you give them a pot that's got just a little bit of extra room. A pot that's too big leaves plants lost and is likely to get waterlogged, since the plant's root system can't drain it.

QUIZ: WHAT TYPE OF HOUSEPLANTS SUIT YOUR PERSONALITY AND LIFESTYLE?

1. **What's your idea of a great night out?**
   (a) A nightclub
   (b) Stargazing in the wilderness
   (c) Sharing a bottle of wine with a few friends
   (d) Listening to some great jazz

2. **Where would you prefer to go on vacation?**
   (a) The beach
   (b) Hiking the woods
   (c) Europe
   (d) India

3. **Which of these describes your lifestyle best?**
   (a) Chaotic
   (b) Natural
   (c) Mellow
   (d) Bohemian

4. **Pick a building:**
   (a) Frank Gehry's MoPOP, Seattle
   (b) Frank Lloyd Wright's Fallingwater
   (c) The Metropolitan Museum of Art
   (d) The Taj Majal

HOW DOES THIS TRANSLATE TO WHICH PLANTS I LIKE?

If you have mostly As, you love the buzz. You need plants that are spectacular, and you probably need them to be low-maintenance, too. The snake plant, with its dramatic blades of leaf, will grow over four feet tall (get the Masoniana variety) and is drought tolerant. Just don't let it get cold; temperatures of under 50F will kill it. You might also consider succulents like the crassulas, with their interesting architectural shapes.

If you have mostly Bs, you're a nature-lover. Fill your home with foliage and turn it into an indoor forest. All kinds of ferns are made for you, and maybe a bamboo palm or two. You might even try your hand at a couple of slightly more difficult-to-grow varieties, since your love of nature will help you understand their needs.

Mainly Cs? You love being surrounded by beautiful things, and you'd rather have a few wonderful plants than a lot of so-so examples. You're certainly the type to give your plants the attention they need. You could pick orchids, or, if you prefer a less tropical vibe, scented pelargoniums; or if you're willing to put the work in, a bonsai tree!

If you have mainly Ds, you have eclectic tastes and you're interested in different places and cultures. Crassula Buddha's Temple is absolutely for you – create a mysterious landscape by planting several of them in a long, shallow container with a few large pebbles. Staghorn fern is another plant you'll love with its huge drooping leaves.

If you find yourself with a mix of A, B, C, and D answers, congratulations! Your diverse preferences suggest that you have a well-rounded personality and enjoy a variety of experiences. This eclectic taste extends to your choice in houseplants as well.

Your ideal indoor garden might include a combination of different plant types, reflecting the different aspects of your personality. Consider incorporating a snake plant for its spectacular and low-maintenance qualities, mirroring the energetic and vibrant side of your personality (like the As). Add some ferns to create an indoor forest, embracing your love for nature (similar to the Bs). Integrate a couple of beautiful and attention-grabbing orchids or scented pelargoniums to satisfy your appreciation for aesthetics and sophistication (as seen in the Cs). Lastly, include Crassula Buddha's Temple or Staghorn fern to bring in an exotic and culturally diverse touch that aligns with your eclectic tastes (similar to the Ds).

In essence, your mix of plant choices will create a harmonious and diverse indoor garden, reflecting the many facets of your vibrant personality and lifestyle. Enjoy the beauty and uniqueness each plant brings to your living space!

That was a fairly light-hearted quiz but it should give you some idea of what direction to look in when you're choosing plants that will fit your personality and lifestyle. But, you'll still need to think about which plants will fit well into your home, so let's take a look at the space you live in and see which plants will be happy to live there.

CHAPTER 2

KEY CONSIDERATIONS: LIGHT, HUMIDITY, DESIGN & LAYOUT

Singer Beth Ditto says that "A beautiful plant is like having a friend around the house" – a lovely sentiment, which shows just how transformative houseplants can be, not just for your home, but for your life.

Even the barest set of four white walls can be turned into an inviting, living environment by simply adding the right plants. They will support your well-being, both physical and emotional, as well as beautifying the space. But to get the most of your houseplants, you need to evaluate the different spaces in your home and find which plants are suited to each space. For instance, a plant that needs full sunlight won't thrive if you put it in a dim corner, and a desert plant like a cactus may not enjoy life in a bathroom or kitchen where it's going to get steamy from time to time.

You'll need to consider various factors. Lighting has a big impact, but you'll also want to think about what else you use certain locations for (don't put a sprawling houseplant on a busy countertop), design elements, and space (lithops takes up almost no space, but a big monstera can dwarf a small room).

 ### THINGS TO CONSIDER

- All plants need light to survive. However, some need more than others; some plants burn in direct light and need a little shade to thrive. Look around your home and see where the light falls at different times of day (grow lights do exist, but it's much easier and cheaper to take advantage of the free resource of sunlight!). Get a light meter app on your smartphone and use it – it might surprise you! It can help to draw a light map of your home. Remember to allow for the impact of roof overhangs and window drapes.

- The direction of light is as important as the amount. Eastern windows get the morning sun, before it gets too hot, which will help maintain humidity. South-facing windows may be too hot in summer, when shade-loving plants could burn, but are great places to put your plants in winter for continuous hours of sunlight. On the other hand, north-facing windows get the least light and heat and get no direct sunlight. West-facing windows get late sunlight, which is less intense than during the earlier part of the day.

- Even in a centrally heated home, there will be some areas that are a little draughty, or that tend to get warm in the afternoon. Putting a plant right next to an outside door will mean it gets a blast of cold air every time you go out or come in. Watch out for over-aggressive aircon use in summer – temperatures below 50F can damage sensitive plants.

- Humidity is important. Most houseplants have tropical origins and like a fairly humid environment, but our homes are usually fairly dry. You can help out by putting plants close together so they create their own microclimate, or using a humidifier, or you could decide to get plants such as cacti that prefer drier surroundings.

- Look for places that a plant can fill without getting in the way. For instance, you can fill corners, though remember the plant will need adequate light. Shelves and windowsills are good places for plants; you can use hanging planters, particularly for trailing plants.

If you've already made a light map, you are well ahead with the next task, which is working out where you would like to put houseplants, and which plants would suit which rooms. For instance, if you want to grow herbs indoors, then it's fairly natural to want to put them in the kitchen. If you want to grow cacti, then a dry, well-lit room is most suitable, for instance a south-facing living room. The bathroom and kitchen are probably equally humid, but most bathrooms have lower light levels, while kitchens tend to have better natural lighting.

PLANTS FOR DIFFERENT ROOMS

LOW LIGHT PLANTS FOR BATHROOMS

The Romans built huge bath complexes wherever they went. But modern architects tend to pack bathrooms into odd corners to optimize the use of space (and of expensive real estate); so you may have a small bathroom, perhaps with no window, or with only a very small window. So you have a room that has low (or no) light, and probably, if everyone takes a shower every morning, quite high humidity.

These are not quite ideal conditions for houseplants. However, plants that are used to growing on the bottom storey of rainforests, in high humidity and hidden from the sun by the tree canopy high above, will cope with them. Bird's nest ferns, blue star ferns, and wood fern, various philodendrons (Xanadu, Pink Princess, Rojo Congo) and mosses are your friends. You can also grow pothos, lucky bamboo, and cast iron plant in these conditions, as well as several draecena, areca palms and kentia palms.

However, there isn't a single houseplant that can do without any light at all (unless you include mushrooms). If your bathroom doesn't have a window, you'll need to keep the door open for indirect light, and perhaps use mirrors to reflect more light. You will also need to rotate plants regularly between your bathroom and another room so they get more natural daylight every so often to give them a boost. If you don't need to put plants in your bathroom, then better not to and put them in rooms that have light.

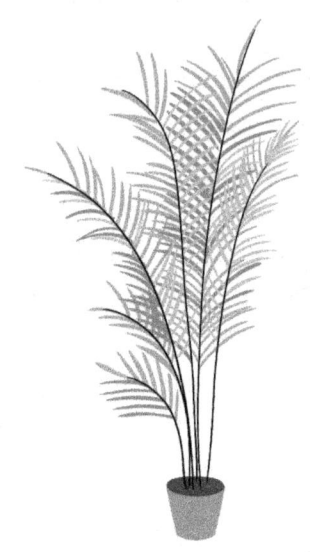

KENTIA PALM

BEDROOM PLANTS

The bedroom is where you may specifically want to put air-purifying plants to improve the environment in which you sleep. The ZZ plant, bamboo palm, and Flamingo lily like indirect light; so does the Swiss cheese plant. Snake plant is a good choice for the bedroom, or you might try succulents, which need a few hours of bright sunlight a day and are easy to care for.

If you want to make a boudoir out of your bedroom, try growing phalaenopsis orchids. These orchids are some of the easiest to grow, and have a three-month flowering season once a year, in the winter; remember, orchids prefer indirect sunlight, so don't put them right on the windowsill (unless it faces north, in which case they'll be fine).

PHALAENOPSIS

LIVING ROOM PLANTS/ DINING ROOM PLANTS

In your living room, you'll probably want at least one larger accent plant to make a statement and complement your décor. Big examples of rubber plants or monstera are a good way to go; fiddle leaf figs are also popular in this role, though they are a bit trickier to get started with.

Alternatively, you could use a number of plants to create a feature such as a bar cart full of foliage (a cart or trolley that you may see in restaurants to deliver drinks to customers – my friend had one of these in their stylish home in Copenhagen), a ladder placed against the wall to train hanging plants on, or a large pot with an interesting planting of different succulents. Look for 'dead space,' such as corners that lack interest. Dead space can be filled with plants, for instance an asparagus fern in a darker corner.

It's sometimes a good idea to try to have different plants in each room. This can help you to differentiate the space. For instance, you might have big snake plants in the living room, but give your dining room a slightly softer feel with trailing pothos and other vines.

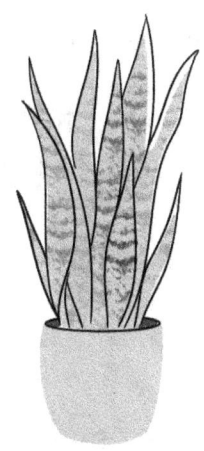

SNAKE PLANT

PLANTS ON BAR TROLLEY

KITCHEN PLANTS

There's nothing to stop you growing cacti or orchids in your kitchen if you want. But it can be really convenient to have fresh herbs growing on your windowsill. Choose the ones you use the most: if you do a lot of Italian cooking, oregano and basil will be your priority, while Asian cuisine fans will want cilantro, green onions, and maybe lemongrass growing in water (just start with a few stalks from the supermarket).

If your kitchen is bright, because the air is likely to be a little more humid than in the living room, all kinds of ferns, air plants, bromeliads and orchids are likely to be happy.

FRESH HERBS

BALCONY PLANTS

If you have a balcony, you can use it to give your houseplants a summer holiday. For some plants, that will put them into overdrive and they'll grow really fast. If you base your balcony planting on temperate evergreens, you can leave gaps for your houseplants, and when you bring them back in for the winter, the balcony won't look bare.

Ferns, ivies, or fatsia japonica with its glossy green leaves are good bases for balcony planting, and hardy to 5F (-15C). Fatsia is not only hardy, it can also tolerate quite a lot of shade. You could then use spring bulbs such as hyacinth, narcissi and tulips to ring the changes, and add lavender or herbs in summer.

For larger balconies, you could grow hydrangeas – green-flowered ones are particularly nice as they look more architectural, almost like a hedge. Jasmine will need a support such as a trellis, and is fast growing, so may need a good pruning from time to time, but it's worth it for the scent that it brings. And bamboo is good for creating a windbreak or privacy screen both on balconies and rooftop gardens, grown in troughs.

You might also consider bay laurel standards or bushes placed in pots. The size of the pot will control the height of the laurel, so you needn't worry about it growing too high.

In summer, why not grow balcony tomatoes and cherries? Tomatoes need a bit more space, and may need support; it's best to choose cherry tomato varieties, which will give you a continual harvest throughout the season. Strawberries grow well in hanging baskets as well as pots; choose varieties with different harvest dates to give you fruit all summer long.

FATSIA JAPONICA

MUNSTEAD

WINDOWSILL PLANTS FOR OUTDOORS

You might decide to save outdoor windowsills for putting your succulents out in the summer. But you might also decide to use temperate climate and frost hardy plants such as boxwood, which can look beautiful if planted in a trough and well-trimmed (beware boxwood caterpillars; you'll need to treat the plant with something like neem oil to keep them off).

Lavender is another choice for windowsills, particularly in a dwarf variety like 'Munstead' or 'Little Lady.' If you prefer bright colors, and have a windowsill in full sun, try rock roses (cistus); the shrub is low and evergreen, and the flowers come in various colors from yellow and white through to pink and mauve.

Finally, areca palm and spider plant are a couple of 'regular' houseplants that will grow happily outside if you fancy a more tropical vibe.

ASSESSING THE LIGHT IN YOUR HOME

Let's put a bit more detail into the lighting aspect now, in terms of assessing exactly what each type of plant needs.

Light gives plants energy; they are fuelled by photosynthesis, processing light, carbon dioxide, and water to create oxygen and energy in the form of sugars. Natural light gives them a mix of wavelengths – importantly, red and blue parts of the spectrum.

The intensity of light is assessed in footcandles (US) or lux/lumens (the rest of the world). One footcandle (1 fc) is the amount of light that would be received by a one square foot surface, one foot away from a (specified) candle. Lux/lumens represent the light that would be received by a surface of one square meter in size, so to convert, multiply footcandles by 10.76 to get lumens. It's a bit difficult to imagine given intensities of light in footcandles, so let's look at some typical situations.

- Full sunlight on a bright day would give you 10,000 fc.
- On an overcast day, you might get only 100 fc.
- A hallway or corridor will usually be lit at just 5-10 fc, since you need just enough light to pass through, not to do anything in particular.
- You might need 200 fc task-lighting in your kitchen or in a graphics studio or small workshop.

That gives you an idea of the kind of intensities we're talking about, but the best way to measure lighting is to use an app which takes a measurement through your smartphone's camera. Ideally, you should take measurements at different times of the day and under different weather conditions so that you get an idea of the highest, lowest, and average values. You should also note how long a particular position gets the light, as some plants need longer hours of sunlight than others.

Light will also be more intense close to windows. Just 5 or 6 feet away from a windowsill in bright direct sunlight, you'll find partly shaded, medium-brightness locations that will work for different plants. If you spot a plant getting sunburned on the tips of its leaves, just moving it a few feet further inside can really help.

You should now be able to divide your home into different areas of light. If you search online, different sources will give different answers for what is considered low, medium and high light in foot candles. According to the American Orchid Society, low would be 1,000-1,500 fc, medium 2,000 and high 3,000. According to The University of Missouri, you should divide your plants into the following light requirements:

- Low light, 50 to 250 fc.
- Medium light, 500 to 1,000 fc.
- High light, over 1,000 fc.

Your eyes are not the best guide to light levels. For instance, you may perceive the difference in your home between a sunny and an overcast day as a slight diminution in available light; but unobstructed sunlight, say on your window sill, can give 10,000 fc, whereas overcast light is just 100 fc – a huge difference!

Indirect light might be filtered by a tree outside, for instance, or by curtains inside. This will give the plant shelter from the full strength of the sun while still giving it high light levels (however, deciduous trees will throw more shade in summer, and much less in winter when their leaves have dropped).

The direction from which the light comes can be important. An east-facing windowsill might get 5,000 fc or more in the morning; a south-facing windowsill in summer could get 10,000 fc; while a north-facing windowsill might get as little as 200 fc, even on a clear day.

Many plants will tolerate low light conditions but grow faster with more light.

Other plants will grow in lower light but won't display the variegated colors on their leaves so well as when they're given more sunlight (it may be a good idea to swap plants around every so often, so that each plant only has to tolerate low light conditions for a month or so at a time). Do remember, too, that most plants need a period of darkness, so ensuring the lights are off or your blackout curtains are closed for eight hours a day is important.

It's always useful to know not just where your plants come from geographically, but their place within their native ecosystem. Forest-floor plants which are used to the shade of the forest canopy will need less light than plants which grow in more open conditions, for instance. Plants with large, dark or fleshy leaves have usually evolved to make best use of low light conditions; most of them will tolerate shade.

The whole business of light metering is fraught. Professional lighting designers often start with a degree in architecture, then specialize. But in your indoor garden, there is only one expert – the houseplant. However much thought you give to your lighting and plant positioning, if a houseplant shows you it's not happy where you've put it or at the amount of light it's getting, you need to listen!

To make life easy for you, I've created a table showing the light conditions that are suitable for the most common houseplants. Most ferns will tolerate low light; most succulents and practically all cacti want bright, direct light. Some plants can be grown with any light, but they may react differently; for instance, hoyas will tolerate low light, but will only grow properly in medium light conditions, and won't flower unless they have bright light to encourage them. Ferns will tolerate low light, but will grow much more satisfactorily given medium light conditions. As for sansevieria, it's not choosy; it will grow in pretty much any light conditions at all.

Light conditions	Plants
Shade / low light	Ferns (e.g., asplenium)
	Peace lilies (may not flower)
	Philodendrons
	Spider plant
	Aluminium plant
	Arrowhead vine
	Cast iron plant
	Chinese evergreen
	Dracaena
	Kentia palm
	ZZ plant
	Snake plant

Light conditions	Plants
Medium light	Asparagus fern (though it will tolerate lower levels of lighting) Peace lilies Jade plant Peperomia (will tolerate low light for a limited period) Pothos Ferns (for better growth) Begonias Ficus, rubber plant Kangaroo vine Dumb cane Ivy (hedera) Citrus (over winter) Philodendrons Majesty palm
High light – indirect	Most herbs Jasmine Aloe vera String of pearls Ti plant Madagascar dragon tree Fiddle leaf fig Bird of paradise Most orchids Sago palm and most other palm trees Snake plant Haworthia
High light – direct	Cacti Basil African milk bush Papyrus Ponytail palm Areca palm Wax agave Common houseleek Flaming Katy Yucca Citrus

WHAT WINDOW PROVIDES THE BEST LIGHT?

There are many things to consider when choosing a window to place your plants near, including size, shade from trees or buildings, direction or overhang. Large windows provide the best growing conditions, as well as those that are not shaded by trees or buildings, and allow you to place the plants further away from them because light will reach them if they are near a big window. But saying that, most plants still need to be within 10 feet of a window.

South facing windows are best where plants need more exposure to light but plants that don't need a lot of direct light may get their leaves burned by too much sun in the summer and spring months. For plants needing less light or that prefer indirect light, you might want to consider putting them in north facing windows.

East and west facing windows are good for plants in the medium light range or that like a few hours of direct morning or afternoon sun.

WAYS OF DEALING WITH NO LIGHT OR VERY LIMITED LIGHT

Most plants will let you know if they are not getting enough light. One of the main signs of this is the growth of long internodes (length of stem between leaves) or the leaves may be smaller than they should be for that plant. Other signs may be pale green stems and foliage or yellowing or drooping leaves.

If you have very limited light in a room, there are various ways of dealing with this. For instance, if you have limited light in one room and medium light in another, you could rotate the plants between rooms on a weekly basis. However, don't transfer low-light plants into bright, sunlit conditions, particularly direct sunlight; that will stress them out.

Adding mirrors and painting the walls white can also help to make the sunlight go further. One reason the cast iron plant was so loved by the Victorians was that nineteenth-century English homes were very dim. Huge swathes of velvet curtain, drapes and fringes on everything, and dark wooden furniture, meant there wasn't a lot of light for growing plants (and of course, if you were a well-to-do plant fancier, you would have had a greenhouse or conservatory for growing your tropical plants).

If this is not enough for the plants you want to grow, you should think about artificial lighting. This is discussed in a later chapter.

MIRROR AND HOUSE PLANT

DESIGNING A PLEASING PLANT LAYOUT

It's important not just to grab some plants and dot them around the place. You should give some thought to designing a layout that you find pleasing.

You may have seen homes where the layout just doesn't work. For instance, a huge loft with a single rubber plant in the corner is just going to make the plant look underpowered. A row of assorted plants in different styled pots on a single windowsill is a sign that there hasn't been much effort employed in thinking where to put the plants. And a single African violet on a mantelpiece tells the story of a Christmas gift that's just managing to hang on to life.

Instead, you could have a complete urban jungle: a vine trailing up the inside of a window to shade your reading nook; a big zinc tray of cacti as an accent for a sunroom; a pot with a snake plant's vertical leaves surrounded by trailing plants, set on a plant stand as a focus for your living room; or a stag horn fern tumbling down the wall of your dining room. If you want inspiration, look at *World of Interiors* or track down Apartment Therapy on the web, or even check out *Architectural Digest*.

Still, my advice would be to start simple. That doesn't mean start small – if you have a huge loft space, buying a tiny lithops isn't going to transform your home! But you might just buy one really big snake plant and put it on a stand in a big copper pot as an attractive accent, or one huge monstera. If you have a mezzanine, you could hang a long planter over the rail and let vine plants hang down into the main space.

Style according to your space. If you have smaller rooms, find smaller or more delicate plants to fill them; it's easy to overwhelm a small bedroom with large, dark-leaved plants. You could put mirrors behind your plants – that gives an illusion that you have double the number of plants, and a lot more space. If you have a huge picture window, you'll need a plant that can fill the space (and likes the sun). If you have a big sofa, find a big plant to stand beside it.

Look at the room analytically. Is there already a focal point like a chimney, a huge window, a spiral staircase? You might want to put even more of an accent there with a plant. Are there dull corners? A plant could liven them up. It can help to make a map, and look at where the gaps are.

You'll also want to select plants to fit your style of interior décor. If you have a bohemian style then vines, trailing plants in macrame hangers, geraniums, and succulents of all kinds could bring even more variety and interest to your home. If your style is more minimalist, then you'll probably choose one or two specimen cacti or statement succulents – a tree houseleek with its huge rosettes might be just right. Is it mid-century modern? Try classic plants for the style such as big rubber plants, ficus, or monstera. Glossy green leaves go well with the bare wood aesthetic. Big, architectural plants also go well with the industrial aesthetic; five different snake plants in a zinc trough could be a great accent for a brick-walled loft, for instance.

If you don't know your style, try one of the interior design quizzes on the internet – there are loads of resources to help you decide whether you'll love a country cottage, industrial, Scandinavian or coastal vibe. Try the quiz at Apartment Therapy, The Ginger Home, or Houzz.

Try to create a focal point. That might be one big plant, like an elephant's ear or a big banana plant, or it might be a 'plant corner,' using a shelving unit to support a vertical garden.

Creating contrasts is another way to liven up your planting. That might mean contrasting different growing styles, such as an upright plant set against a background of trailing vines; different heights; or different leaf shapes, for instance the sharpness of a snake plant's blades set against the rounded leaves of jade plants or the delicate shapes of ferns.

If you're interested in interior decoration, you've probably heard of the rule of three – using three objects together to create a cluster, such as three different bowls on a side table. You could cluster three succulents together in a single pot, or you could put three contrasting plants together (a cactus, a vine, and a fern, for instance). Other odd numbers also work well: line up five planters, and it makes a definite set, whereas six looks as if you could carry on adding *ad infinitum*. Don't ask why – that's the way our minds work!

On the other hand, in some cases you'll want to ignore the rule of three and go for symmetry. For instance if you have a room with a big central chimneypiece, you could use two tall, matching plants, one each side, to balance the composition. You could also use matching plants to 'guard' a door, but you'll only want to do this in a fairly formal space. It would work in a grand Paris apartment but not in a log cabin!

You might want to layer plants at different heights, with some in high hanging planters, some on the floor, some on windowsills or side tables. It's probably best if you build a layered design from the ground up: start at floor level with the biggest plants, and with plants on high planters, to make a statement, then add the smaller plants. You can use different sized planters to put similarly sized plants at different heights, too.

Making a vertical accent can be done with tall plants but it can also be done with trailing plants or with plants that climb trellises. You can also use shelves but don't put them too high or the plants will be difficult to access for watering. And you can use plant hangers to let vines trail down in the middle of a room; this can create a canopy effect or even be used as a room divider. You could even hang epiphytic plants such as air plants by fine, almost invisible filaments so they appear to be floating in the air.

Don't forget to use color proactively. Dark purples and greenish yellows are common; if you want neon yellow and pink, you may have to look a bit harder, but you can find really bright colors in bromeliads and some cacti. You might choose colorful flowers like begonias and African violets, but you can do a lot with bright leaves – the croton variety 'Bush on Fire' is bright gold and will pick up any room you put it into.

Here are just a few suggestions for colored varieties of common houseplants:

COLORED VARIETIES

- Caladium (elephant ears) - 'Florida Sweetheart' in bright pink, 'Bombshell' with dark pink inside bordered by green, and 'Red Frill.'
- Philodendron 'Black Cardinal,' 'Rojo Congo,' 'Imperial Red,' 'Prince of Orange.'
- Cordyline 'Firebrand' and 'Rubra' (red).
- Ficus elastica (rubber plant) 'Burgundy,' 'Tineke' (green, cream, pink), 'Ruby,' 'Red Ruby.'
- Red moon cactus.

PLANTERS

Remember that the planters can be as important to your décor as what you plant in them. Use stands and planters to promote your plants and fit your style. For instance, you could use a bamboo stand, occasional table, glass shelf, a ladder with pots slung from the rungs; you could group plants on a table, put them on a room divider in an open plan living room, or use a trellis for trailing plants.

You could use any of the following as planters (though you will need to either use a regular pot inside, or provide a drainage hole by carefully drilling one):

PLANTERS

- Old enamel cups.
- Big copper pots.
- An old brown teapot.
- A cake tin.
- White ramekin dishes (for small succulents).
- Jugs.
- Zinc buckets.
- Mason jars (with gravel and charcoal drainage in the bottom).
- A wicker basket holding different pots.
- A basket lined with plastic.
- An old watering can.
- A wooden cutlery tray.
- Glass terrine pots.
- Beer glasses.
- A biscuit tin holding small pots.
- Old yogurt pots.
- An old wooden crate (don't forget to line it).
- Handmade cement planters.
- Recycled paint cans or Coke cans (you can sandpaper the paint off for a simple metallic effect).
- Cereal bowls.
- A battered saucepan.
- Teacups.
- Wire mesh in a frame for holding bromeliads or air plants.
- Old rubber boots.
- Shadow boxes.
- Tea tins.
- A Pyrex oven dish.
- Vintage urns.
- A glass vase.
- Old casseroles.
- Driftwood (for succulents or epiphytes).

ZINC BUCKET PLANTER

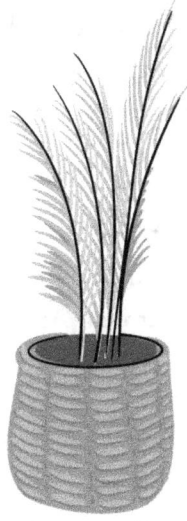

WICKER BASKET PLANTER

The traditional terracotta pot has advantages. Terracotta absorbs water quickly and so helps to prevent the pot becoming waterlogged. If terracotta pots fit your farmhouse style, that's great; but otherwise, you can use cache-pots or planters to hide them.

SUMMARY — HOW TO PLACE YOUR PLANTS

- Start simple.
- Style according to your space.
- Look at the room analytically.
- Select plants to fit your style of interior décor.
- Try an interior design online quiz for ideas.
- Try to create a focal point.
- Create contrasts.
- Think about the rule of three or go for symmetry.
- Make a vertical accent.
- Layer plants at different heights.
- Use color proactively.
- Think about which planters will look best.

Let your imagination free. As well as traditional planters, you could create a terrarium using a large bottle or planting under a glass dome, you could create a mini-greenhouse, or even a living room pergola. Take a look around your house for things that could be made into plant containers. You may be surprised what you can do; one plant enthusiast has even re-used a vintage pram!

Of course, you can also buy plenty of magnificent planters in the stores or online. In fact, trawling around Amazon or Etsy, even if you don't buy anything, could give you some great ideas.

You should think about color when you're getting your containers. If all your plants are simple green varieties, then you can introduce color by using brightly painted or glazed pots. If you have a bunch of variegated and colored plants, then you might decide to go for white or metallic containers to keep things simple at root level.

 ## DOS AND DON'TS

DOs

- Decide on the 'look' before you decide which plants to buy.
- Try to find plants that can complement each other in a cluster, or that contrast.
- Try different treatments in different rooms, such as hanging pots in the kitchen, trees in pots in the

living room, a couple of shelves of pots in the bathroom.
- If you want lots of small plants, find a way to bring them together creatively, for instance, planting them all inside a big terrarium.

DON'TS

There are a few don'ts when it comes to houseplants.

- Don't stick lots of tiny pots on the windowsill. Three bigger plants would look better, or if you want a variety of plants, hold the pots in a larger planter.
- Don't forget that plants grow! If you buy a fast-growing plant, remember it will take up more space next year than it does now.
- Don't clutter! Less is more – unless you're going for the home jungle look.
- Don't limit yourself to one plant per pot.
- Don't use fake plants!
- Don't have all the same height and shape of plant.

 ## OTHER CONSIDERATIONS

Containers often look good with three plants in. You might want to adopt the 'thriller, filler, spiller' method – one accent plant, one plant that fills up the space, and one plant that trails out of the pot. Make sure, though, that the three plants you use have the same watering, feeding and light requirements.

The Japanese are well-known for having developed bonsai trees, which are kept tiny by heavy pruning. Bonsai takes a lot of experience and a lot of hard work to get right, and isn't recommended unless you are capable of being really obsessive about it. But now, Japanese designers have created the next best thing to bonsai, miniature landscapes made of succulents. Cacti and succulents are huge in Japan, so check out Japanese growers' Instagrams for ideas; ateliertokiiro is a great place to start.

How many plants should you have? That's rather a "how long is a piece of string" question, but we could start with a much-quoted NASA study that suggested you'd want two big, leafy plants for every 100 square feet if you just wanted them as air purifiers[4]. Another study, from RMIT University in Melbourne, Australia, advocates ten plants for a regular sized living room (200 square feet), though it doesn't specify size (if you want air freshener plants, remember to choose plants with large leaf surfaces)[5].

Size is important, of course. If you choose orchids or smaller succulents, you might want more individual plants, but the overall volume would probably be the same as with two or three big rubber plants.

---

[4] https://spinoff.nasa.gov/Spinoff2019/cg_7.html
[5] https://www.bhg.com.au/how-many-plants-you-need-per-room

It's easier to tell how many plants is too many. If any of these things are happening, you may have too many plants or you just need a larger home:

- Your home has become much too humid.
- You can't move for plants.
- They're dying because you can't look after them.

However, if you're just getting started, hopefully it will take you a while until any of these situations become a problem!

QUIZ: WHAT'S YOUR STYLE?

1. **When you get home, what do you want your home to feel like?**
   a) Relaxing.
   b) Interesting.
   c) Cool.
   d) Friendly.
2. **If you had your choice, you'd live in:**
   a) a beach house or log cabin.
   b) a townhouse.
   c) a modern loft-style apartment.
   d) a sprawling family house.
3. **You have to pick one of these colors for your sofa. Which one do you choose?**
   a) Ocean blue.
   b) Fuchsia pink.
   c) Black.
   d) Rusty red.
4. **What would you rather drink?**
   a) Hot chocolate.
   b) Jasmine-infused Chinese green tea.
   c) Double espresso.
   d) Apple juice.
5. **Your ideal dinner guest is**
   a) A friend you spend lots of time with.
   b) Someone with a fascinating life that you haven't met before.
   c) An Instagram influencer.
   d) Family.

Mainly A? You should probably think about a Scandinavian, coastal, or farmhouse look, with lots of light colors and bright accents, plenty of wood and perhaps some vintage furniture. Your plants will help the place feel lived-in and laid-back, so concentrate on filling corners and windowsills, and use trailing plants or hanging planters to break up the space.

Mainly B means you should look at a Bohemian style, or maybe shabby chic or eclectic; lots of colors and different periods thrown into the mix. You can put any kind of plants into this environment, but you need to mix them up, with plenty of layering, too. Pick the most interesting plants you can find, and try pairing them with unusual containers.

Mainly C, and you might be minimalist or mid-century modern, or – just possibly – industrial. You're going to need a few strong plants, full of character, that can hold their own against your strong design style.

If you answered mainly D, you're going to want a rustic or farmhouse/cottage style, and you'll want plenty of plants around. Filling a shelf with plants or using mason jars to hold tiny succulent gardens are both good ideas for you – and you'll want some colorful flowering plants to bring joy into the interior.

If you find yourself with a mix of A, B, C, and D answers, your style is likely an eclectic blend that draws inspiration from various design aesthetics. Your home reflects a harmonious fusion of relaxation, interest, coolness, and friendliness. Here's how you can translate this diverse style into your plant choices:

- Combine Scandinavian, coastal, or farmhouse elements (like the As) with lots of light colors, bright accents, and vintage furniture. Your plant selections should complement this by creating a laid-back and lived-in feel. Focus on filling corners and windowsills with a variety of plants, and consider using trailing plants or hanging planters to break up the space.
- Embrace a Bohemian, shabby chic, or eclectic style (similar to the Bs) that incorporates lots of colors and different periods. Your plant choices can be equally diverse, with an emphasis on interesting and unique plants. Mix them up with various types and use unusual containers to add a layer of creativity to your space.

If you have minimalist, mid-century modern, or industrial tendencies (like the Cs), opt for strong plants with character that can hold their own against your bold design style. Choose plants with clean lines and distinctive features to complement the sleek and modern aesthetic of your home.

For those with a rustic or farmhouse/cottage style (similar to the Ds), incorporate plenty of plants around your space. Consider filling shelves with plants or using mason jars to create tiny succulent gardens. Add colorful flowering plants to bring joy and vibrancy to the interior, enhancing the warm and welcoming atmosphere of your home.

In essence, your mix of styles can be beautifully reflected in your plant choices, creating a unique and personalized indoor environment that seamlessly blends relaxation, interest, coolness, and friendliness. Enjoy curating your diverse and stylish living space!

By now you should have a good idea of what plants you want to choose and where you want to put them. In the next part of the book, we're going to look at how to look after your plants from day-to-day to make sure they're healthy and looking their best.

STEP 2
DAY-TO-DAY PLANT CARE ROUTINES

CHAPTER 3
BASIC PLANT CARE & MAINTENANCE

My friend Charley loves her houseplants. She's even given some of them names. She puts pictures of them on Instagram and calls herself their 'plant mom.' Because she rents, she's moved home several times since I've known her, but the plants always go along too (they even moved back to Mom and Dad's at one point when she was between rentals).

But she worries every time she goes off on vacation that her plants won't survive. She has to find a plant-minder, and she writes out a list of exactly what each plant needs, and when – and that's just for a long weekend! She often has to work odd hours, too, and it's sometimes difficult for her to give her plants the attention they need. It's sad that the plants she loves stress her out so much. How could she make life easier for herself?

That's the question this chapter aims to address. You may have an idea that looking after houseplants is crazily difficult and time-consuming. While it's true that there are some houseplants that will drive you insane with their demands, some basic knowledge coupled with a basic routine, and maybe some smart automation, will let you look after most of the common plants successfully. The trick is to create a simple routine that works both for you and for your plants.

First of all, pick the right plants and put them in the right place. If you're a beginner, why choose plants that will give you a hard time?

You'll see that plenty of names, like croton and pothos, apply to plant families with a lot of different varieties available. So if you've learned to keep golden pothos nice and healthy, you could add a bit of brightness to your home by getting a neon pothos with its yellow leaves or try the white-fringed 'Pearls and Jade' pothos or stunningly dramatic 'Snow Queen.' While some of these plants have slightly different preferences – for instance, neon pothos likes a bit more light than the regular variety – the family as a whole behave in similar ways, so you know what to expect.

You'll see that the 'easy' column has a lot more names than the other two columns, which is a good sign. The easiest plants of all are marked with an asterisk.

Easy/*Almost indestructible	Slightly picky	Temperamental/Difficult
*Pothos	Maranta	Fiddle-leaf fig
*Cast iron plant	(prayer plant)	Air plants
*Snake plant	Parlor palm	Bird's nest fern
Chinese evergreen	Chinese	Staghorn fern
*Ponytail palm	money plant	Carnivorous
*Lucky bamboo	Elephant's ear	plants – Venus flytrap,
*Rubber plant	African violet	pitcher plant, sundews
*English ivy	Peace Lily	
*Swiss cheese plant	Aloe vera	
Yucca	Begonia	
Flaming Katy	Dragon tree	
Flamingo flower	Bromeliad	
Asparagus fern	Croton	
Haworthia	Phalaenopsis	
Baby rubber plant	orchid	
*Spider plant	Banana tree	
Philodendron	Boston fern	
Christmas cactus	Prayer plant	
*ZZ Plant	Nerve plant	
Snake plant		
Inch plant/Spiderwort		
Corn plant		
Cacti		
*Jade plant		
Areca palm		

Chapter 2 already talked about plants which want higher light levels, or more shade. Try to buy plants for specific spaces, so that you don't end up with too many bright light loving plants to go on your one south-facing windowsill. If you're buying plants which will go into a bathroom with no direct light, think of a shady but better-lit space in your home where they can be put every couple of weeks on rotation, and double up.

The two things you need to avoid are plants not getting any light at all, and plants getting badly sunburned. In between the two extremes, you'll be able to see whether plants need a bit more or a bit less light, and you can simply move them, put up a muslin curtain to shield them from bright daylight, or get a grow light to give them a bit more exposure. Having a schedule for checking on your plants, even if you only have a small apartment, is sensible, so you don't miss any signs of plant stress.

Once you've chosen your plants for each of your light zones, the first step in caring for them is to give them the other long-term conditions they need: the right temperature, the right humidity, and the right soil and nutrients.

TEMPERATURE, HUMIDITY, SOIL AND NUTRIENTS

TEMPERATURE AND HUMIDITY

Most houseplants need temperatures around 60-75F (15-24C). That's where most of us tend to keep our domestic and office heating, too. However, you might have problems if there is one room you don't heat, such as a mudroom, or an entrance hall that's drafty. Cold can kill a plant very quickly. Houseplants also don't like it too hot indoors. It's actually a bigger problem for houseplants than it is for plants growing outside, since the air is likely to be dry, and there are no cooling breezes. In summer, even if your home as a whole is reasonably cool, a south-facing window could give your plants too much heat to handle.

Humidity can also make a big difference to a plant's health. Misting or placing a pebble tray filled with water under your plants can help if the atmosphere is too dry, but plants with really high humidity requirements ought to be in the bathroom or kitchen, or perhaps in a closed terrarium.

SOIL

Soil is a factor that a lot of beginner houseplant parents forget. 'Any old dirt' will not do, even for the easy-to-grow plants! Store-bought houseplant compost will suit most houseplants; don't use garden compost, which isn't designed to drain as well and may not contain the right mix of nutrients. Adding perlite, coco coir or vermiculite can help the soil drain, which is ideal for houseplants which generally like their roots relatively dry (that's most of them). For cacti and succulents, which are desert plants, you could add perlite, or you could mix some horticultural grit into the compost; or you could buy special cactus growing medium. Ferns, terrariums and orchids also have special requirements.

It's worth having a soil thermometer so that you can take the soil temperature. If the soil is too cold (below 15C or 60F), that could slow down a plant's metabolic processes; that means it will grow more slowly, may not have flowers, or will flower late. If the soil is too hot (above 24C or 75F), the plant may lose too much water, and start to wilt. Soil that's too warm is also likely to harbor maleficent microorganisms, such as those that cause root rot. The same is true for all house plants.

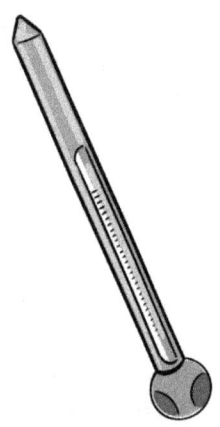

SOIL THERMOMETER

So how can you control the soil temperature? One way is to water a little more often if you need to cool it down, or keep it drier in order to warm it up. You might also want to repot the plant, if it is filling its pot, since larger containers don't heat up so quickly. You could use a heat mat, or you could just move the plant!

NUTRIENTS

Although plants get most of their energy from the sun through photosynthesis, they all need various other nutrients, which they pull from the earth. Growing mediums contain enough nutrients for a month or two but then the nutrients need to be replenished. In the wild, there would be fallen leaves, earthworms, and microorganisms in the soil, all doing their bit to provide more nutrients; with your houseplants, you need to take on the task of giving your plants a feed every so often.

Different plants have different requirements. Some will need a little fertilizer every couple of weeks. Make sure, if you have fast-growing plants, that they get what they need, as growth takes food (if you have a teenager, you already know this!). Others may only need monthly feeding, and some plants only need feeding in the growing season (spring to fall). Your plant label should contain this information, and you don't want to lose it. It's worth taking a photo of the plant label on your smartphone so you always have the information to hand.

Plants will also want repotting from time to time. This both gives them a new pot with room to accommodate their recent growth and gives them fresh soil with fresh nutrients in it. It's best to repot in spring, so the plant is just getting into growth mode when you repot it.

The right size pot is important. Don't leave too much space, but don't cramp your plant's style; it needs just a little room all the way around. It's just like sizing clothes; you don't want clothes that are too tight, but equally you don't want to be wearing clothes so loose that you look as if you're wearing a tent!

WATERING A HOUSE PLANT

 ## WATERING

Watering is the most common cause of plant murder! So it's really important to get it right.

You can kill a plant by watering it in one of two ways:

1. You forget to water it at all, and eventually it dries up.
2. You water it too much. The soil in the pot becomes boggy, the plant starts rotting, and eventually its roots rot away.

Now we all know instinctively that we can kill plants by giving them no water at all, so the first mistake is one that's only made by very forgetful gardeners. Far more common is the second method of plant murder, overwatering. That's because we think "this plant will die if I don't water it," so we keep watering it so that it won't die. By trying not to kill it, you kill it!

There will be some much more specific advice on watering in the next chapter, but for now, just remember every plant has its particular needs, and they're likely to be for less water rather than more.

 ## EACH PLANT HAS ITS OWN NEEDS

So now let's look at what special care individual houseplants will need. First of all, let's take the 'easy' list.

EASY PLANTS

Perhaps the most important thing to understand is that most plants fall into one of two main types. There are those that do not like to have their roots waterlogged, and some that like to dry out fully between waterings. And there are those that prefer the soil to be moist, though very few plants like to sit with their roots in water. Make sure you know which kind of plant is which. If you want to make your life really easy, get plants that all belong to the same group, so you only have to remember one schedule and get used to caring for those particular plants. Or color-code your plants blue for watering, and red for drying out first.

Some easy-care plants include the Yucca plant and the Jade plant – see the Plant Directory in the back of the book for details of such plants.

YUCCA PLANT

JADE PLANT

MODERATELY CHALLENGING PLANTS

Have a look over the easy to care for plants in the Appendix and you'll see they vary from the totally indestructible to those that have a few special conditions. The moderately challenging plants have rather more special conditions to meet, but if you have already got a little experience with easy houseplants, there's nothing you won't be able to cope with.

Some moderately challenging plants include the Dragon Tree and the Boston Fern – check them out in the Plant Directory at the back of the book.

DRAGON TREE

BOSTON FERN

 ## DIFFICULT PLANTS

Now let's look at why the 'difficult' plants are so challenging. Some of these plants will really exercise your skills!

FIDDLE-LEAF FIG

This is choosy. It needs humidity and bright, but indirect, light. It burns easily in direct sunlight. It needs to be rotated every few days so that it grows evenly, otherwise it will develop a pronounced leaning toward the light. For humidity, it will need misting and a pebble tray filled with water under the pot, or a humidifier – it likes things steamy, steamier than your living room, without a doubt. It's even choosy about fertilizer, preferring a '3-1-2' mix (three parts nitrogen to one of phosphorous and two of potassium) rather than a 'balanced' ('10-10-10' or '20-20-20') mix.

FIDDLE-LEAF FIG

Its leaves need to be dusted every couple of weeks. And while it is happy with ordinary compost for soil, it's very picky about how much watering it wants – not enough, and it will wilt; too much, and it may develop root rot. It's also sensitive to salt levels in the soil, so it needs the soil flushed every month (at least) to get rid of salt build-up.

And it doesn't like drafts. Plus it needs high nitrogen fertilizer. This plant isn't impossible to grow, but you'll need to indulge its whims.

There's just one thing that *is* easy to do with a fiddle-leaf fig. Propagating the plant from stem cuttings is really, really simple.

AIR PLANTS

You might be surprised to see air plants on the 'difficult' list. They live in the air, requiring no watering or soil, so surely they must be easy to keep?

The difficulty is that they need good air circulation and regular misting. Tap water won't do; you'll need to use distilled water or rainwater, because the salts in softened water will upset them. They need a special fertilizer, which doesn't contain urea nitrogen, as well. They won't tolerate drafts, they need a relatively high temperature (60F and above), and they need bright but indirect light.

A different way of watering air plants is to dunk them in water two or three times a week, but they then need to be shaken out so no water pools in the middle of the plant. If they stay damp, they can start to rot.

None of these difficulties are insurmountable, but they make air plants high maintenance.

BIRD'S NEST FERN

This fern is worth growing for its ability to survive in very low light levels and its beautiful, rippled leaves. Its difficulty comes mainly from the fact that it needs soil as moist as it can be *without* being waterlogged, and that's a really tough call to make. It's particularly tough if you don't have much experience of houseplants. It needs a half-strength fertilizer every few months – it's not a big feeder. Misting and mulching can help, but the thing that will help you the most is getting some experience with more tolerant ferns before taking on the bird's nest.

STAGHORN FERN

Staghorn fern, like the air plants, is epiphytic – it attaches itself to a tree, but doesn't use the wood for its food. It doesn't need a lot of light, but like the bird's nest fern, it needs to be kept moist consistently, and it needs monthly feeding with balanced fertilizer. Take the mess factor into account before you hang a staghorn fern on the wall of your living room! Its desire for continual moisture also makes it a difficult plant if your lifestyle involves frequent travel.

BEGONIA

Begonia can be either easy or challenging. It can be a very, very easy plant to keep, just as long as you're prepared to see it go to houseplant heaven after a year. Lots of people have a begonia just for the flowers, and then treat it as disposable.

If you want to become a real begonia parent, you need to deadhead the plant to keep it healthy, taking off all the dying flowers. You'll need to give it a high-nitrogen fertilizer every two weeks once it starts to flower. You'll also need to keep it continually moist, and protect it from drafts, *and* give it indirect light, for instance, in a west-facing window. So that's quite a job.

BEGONIA

CARNIVOROUS PLANTS

Carnivorous plants are always fun for the kids. My grandad had a Venus flytrap, and I spent ages watching it, in case it ever decided to eat a fly (it never did). But they need watering every single day – they're just about the only houseplant that's happy when its roots are wet. And disappointingly, these plants often die down to ground level in winter, making them rather boring.

CREATING A PLANT CARE ROUTINE THAT WORKS FOR YOU

So far, I've been talking about what each plant needs. But you also need to think about your own lifestyle and preferences. You might be the kind of person who wants a simple daily maintenance job. You might prefer to do your plant maintenance intensively at the weekend. You may be a scatty person who needs reminders, or a disciplined person who finds it easier to commit to an early morning watering appointment in your daily diary.

But you do need a routine. That's a given. Fortunately, there are various ways you can make that routine much easier to keep up.

HOW TO CREATE A ROUTINE

- Do it for you, not for Instagram.
- Start with a routine you know is going to be achievable (just like you started with easy plants to look after).
- Have goals. A simple goal: "I want to have three plants and not kill any of them this year." A less simple goal: "propagate enough succulents to give all my friends one for a holiday gift." Remember why you wanted to have houseplants, and what space you want them to occupy in your life.
- Be prepared. Read up on plants, get the right pots and containers, get the fertilizers and compost that you need, get a mister, trowel, other tools.
- Write down your routine. That makes it real. It also helps you keep consistent.
- Have a visual way of checking off your routine, such as a tickbox checklist. Visual reminders, such as a "Have you watered the plants?" note on the back of your front door, can be useful.

When you're thinking of goals, you might also want to create a goal of how you want to *feel*. For instance, you might say "I want to feel surrounded by life," or "I want to feel that I can nurture something," or "I want my life to feel brighter." You might say "I want to feel I have something beautiful in my home." That's something to work towards, just as much as a more practical goal.

It can be helpful if you try to find a slot that's already open in your schedule and put your plant maintenance routine there.

If you work from home one day a week, your lunchtime break might become plant time, for instance. Or if you're often out in the evenings, but live close to work and exercise at lunchtime, then early morning might be your best time.

Don't be afraid to use technology to help you stick to your routine. You might set a weekly alarm for feeding those hungry African violets, or a daily alarm to check on your plants. You could use Google Assistant to remind you when you need to water or add fertilizer.

You might also get support from friends and family. When I started out, I didn't know anyone else with houseplants. Now, I have plenty of people I can ring if I have a problem with a plant that I can't fix, or want to track down a different variety of a plant. I even have people who buy me new plants for my birthday! If you can buddy up with another plant parent you can learn the ropes together, commiserate when you have the occasional failure, and celebrate your successes.

Consistency is important, in two ways. It's obviously important for your plants, which will get used to the right routine. But it's also important for you – it should give you a sense of confidence and pride that you're able to keep your plants in good condition and know immediately if one of your plants is under the weather.

Keep things balanced. When you decided to have houseplants, you didn't envisage giving up your social life for them, or never going on vacation again. Remember that your plants are there for you; they should be a source of contentment, not a source of stress. If you find that keeping that temperamental fiddle leaf fig in condition is taking up all your time and occupying your mind, then maybe it's time to get a nice easy-to-live-with monstera to put in its place. Make sure that your daily routine is planned in such a way that the rest of your life doesn't get put on the back burner.

I highly recommend the excellent article on fanatic collectors of nepenthe (pitcher plants) in *Wired* magazine (it's in the reading list). I think it's actually quite sad to read how obsessive some of these people become, particularly when you realize how that obsession feeds into illegal harvesting of plants and endangers the species in the wild. So you might want to try to stay grounded, even if you do find there's something addictive about certain species.

You might want to think about writing a routine for each individual plant, too. It's easy to do while your collection is still small, and helps you get used to different species' different needs.

DIFFERENT ROUTINES

Daily
My daily routine goes like this:

- "Hello sunshine!" A moment to look outside and welcome the light into my life.
- Misting my humidity-loving plants a little.
- Checking on the soil for plants that like frequent watering.
- Feeling the foliage and spending a little time with each plant, just to spot any early signs of distress.
- Picking one plant to appreciate and taking the time to look at it from different angles.

Weekly
My weekly routine goes like this:

- Checking all the plants for watering (but only watering them if they need it).
- Taking my scissors and trimming, pruning, or deadheading if it's needed, taking off any dead leaves.
- Rotation – turning plants around on their axis, just a tiny amount, and also rotating low-light plants between the bathroom and the spare bedroom so they all get their turn at having some natural light.
- Dusting the leaves.

Monthly
A good monthly routine would definitely include dusting. And it should also include a feed of fertilizer (though not in the winter), and a thorough check for pests, and rotation of some of the bigger plants.

Seasonal
Then there are activities you'll want to carry out seasonally:

- Repotting if necessary (if the roots are coming out of the pot, or growth is slowing down). Generally, you'll want to do this in spring, which means plants get a new pot just as they are going to start growing into it.
- Change to the winter regime – most plants need less watering and feeding when they are not in growing season.
- Kick-starting your plants in spring – water them more, feed them up, and check if they are in sunlight that's now too strong.
- If you repotted, that new soil contains the nutrients the plant needs for the first month or so; otherwise plants will need fertilizer as a 'multivitamin'-style boost.
- Remember to adjust for the sunlight every few months as the sun is higher or lower in the sky and reaches different places in the room.

YOUR BASIC EQUIPMENT

The most important discipline here is to keep your tools handy all the time. Don't tuck them away in a cupboard and forget about them. Having a little portable carrier with all your tools in can also really help, particularly if you have a lot of different rooms to look after.

You need a watering can. To be specific, you need a watering can with a long spout. This lets you direct the water to the bottom of the plant, rather than watering the leaves (a lot of plants don't like getting their leaves wet). It also means you don't have to bend down to water floor-level plants.

You'll need a plant mister or spray bottle for two purposes. One is helping plants that like high humidity, though the jury is out on how much it will help them (finding them a more humid space to live would be better). The other is spraying the leaves with various mixtures to get rid of bugs.

You'll want to get some fertilizers. The nutrients in the potting mix will only last a month or so, and your plants don't have access to a natural source of nutrients. You can certainly look for organic fertilizers, if you want to reduce your carbon footprint, but you're going to need to give *some* fertilizer to your plants. For most plants it will be a 'balanced' fertilizer, but for some (such as cacti and orchids) you may be better off buying a specialized feed. You may decide to go for liquid feed, which gives you total control of how much you give the plant, or to use a slow-release plant spike, which has the advantage of lasting a season without you having to worry about feeding schedules.

You'll need pots, and the pots will need drainage holes (if they don't have one, drill one, or use gravel and charcoal as a drainage medium at the bottom of the pot). You'll then need to block the drainage hole; a good way is with custom made drainage discs which let water out while keeping the dirt in. You'll also need a saucer or tray underneath to catch any water that drains out!

Pruning scissors are needed for trimming your houseplants. Keep them separate from your kitchen scissors and keep them sharp and sterile. Short-bladed pruning snips are worth getting, as you have a comfortable hold but the blade is not long enough to catch other plants or leaves by mistake.

A small shovel and trowel are needed for repotting, and it's worth getting a pair of stout gardening gloves for prickly or toxic plants. For instance, you really don't want to get euphorbia sap on your skin, so wearing gloves for repotting them is good common sense.

Finally, you need a plant brush (for cacti and succulents). You could buy a special brush, or you could just use an old toothbrush.

I like to keep three well-labeled squeezy bottles in my toolbox, one with rubbing alcohol or neem oil, one with bleach, and one with dish soap and water. This lets me keep my tools clean and my plants clean – if I see any pests, they get the rubbing alcohol treatment. I also keep a pack of tissues in the box for wiping leaves down afterwards. The bleach is there for sterilizing tools in between different plants.

Neem oil is worth buying as a really good, natural way of getting rid of pests. I find I don't use it as often as I do the alcohol and the soapy water, so it only comes out when I decide to do a mass spraying.

We already talked about pots and planters, but you may need plant supports such as bamboo stakes, trellis, or moss poles. I like to make sure my bamboo stakes are safe by putting a little Pokemon pencil topper on each of them; that way, no one's going to get poked in the eye. You might also want to think about cork mats or coasters to go under pots and prevent water stains on furniture.

Moving into more sophisticated tools, you might want to buy a moisture meter. You can always use your finger to measure the moisture in the soil, but if you're starting out, this can be tricky, so having a moisture meter takes the guesswork out of the job. It will help you develop a good instinct so that eventually you'll be able to use your fingers with good accuracy.

A humidity meter for measuring the humidity in the air is useful, too. It may be combined with a thermometer so you can read off the temperature at the same time. Remember that the humidity in different places in the same room can be different, as can the temperature. You'll need to use the meter close up to the plant to get the right reading, though sticking one on the fridge is a good way to remind yourself of overall humidity levels. Some cheap meters have poor quality control, so it may be worth moving upmarket a bit. However, you only need a relative humidity (RH) reading, not absolute humidity or dew point readings, which are more useful to large-scale greenhouse growers.

Smart temperature sensors are now available in little pucks (like a hockey puck) that you put next to a plant, and will report to your smartphone. Perhaps that's overkill but it's a neat idea and they are not all that expensive.

If you want to grow plants with high humidity needs, you might want to think about getting a plant humidifier. Ultimately, this is much more effective than a pebble tray or misting. I'd suggest, though, that you want to wait and see if your houseplant journey is leading you in that direction before you think about humidifiers.

You might also want grow lights. Even if the light in your home is usually enough for your plants, having a few portable grow lights can help you through the winter, or perk up a plant that for whatever reason hasn't had enough sunlight recently.

Your life right now is going to be about looking after the plants you have. But later on, you'll learn how to propagate plants, so it's worth thinking about a propagation kit. If you want to propagate in water, you'll need test tubes or narrow necked glass containers; kits are available quite cheaply. You'll also want to get some hormone rooting powder, which helps stimulate the plants to develop their root systems.

SUMMARY OF BASIC EQUIPMENT NEEDED

Basic equipment

- Watering can.
- Plant mister – for helping plants that like high humidity and for bug control.
- Specialist feed or fertilizer.
- Pots with drainage holes.
- Pruning scissors.
- Trowel and shovel.
- Stout gardening gloves.
- Plant brush.
- Three bottles – bleach, soap and water, rubbing alcohol.
- Neem oil.
- Plant supports.
- Cork mats or coasters.

More sophisticated equipment

- Moisture meter.
- Humidity meter.
- Thermometer.
- Smart temperature sensor.
- Plant humidifier.
- Grow lights.
- Propagation kit.

WATERING CAN

PLANT MISTER

POTS WITH DRAINAGE HOLES

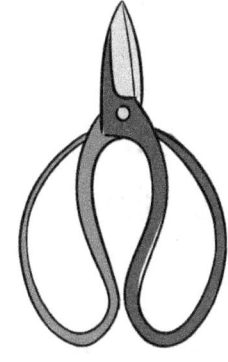
PRUNING SCISSORS

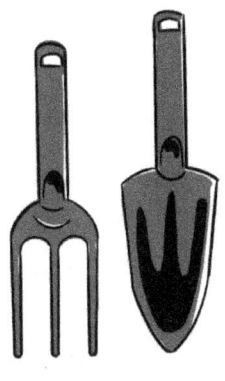
TROWEL AND SHOVEL

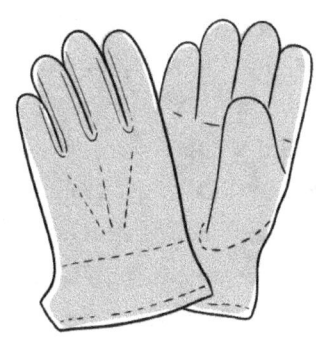
STOUT GARDENING GLOVES

LEAF CLEANING BRUSH

CORK MATS

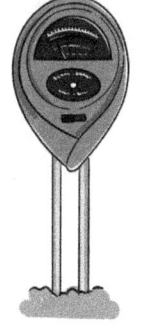
MOISTURE METER

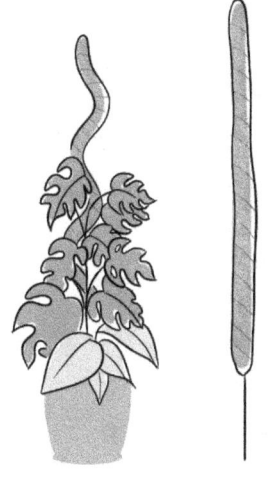
PLANT SUPPORT

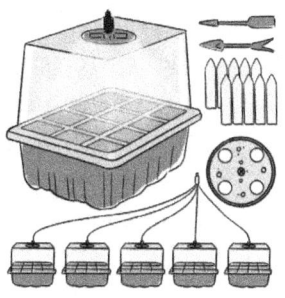
PROPAGATION KIT

HEATING

You probably have your own opinion on how warm your home should be. Most of us have! The only problem is that you may not share that preference with your plants.

Fortunately, it's easy to arrange things so you *and* your plants are happy. If you're not heating a particular room, or if the temperature is a little lower than your particular plants like, you can get a heat mat. You could also get directional heaters, but they are bulky; I find heat mats are a more discreet way of providing a temperature boost. They also have the benefit of not creating drafts.

HEAT MAT

If you are just worried about temperatures falling while you're out, you could use Google Home and a smart plug to get the mat to come on if the temperature drops below a certain level.

If you're really geeky, you really ought to take a look at some of the ideas for automation on hackaday.com for automating your indoor garden. For instance, you could 3D-print a plant pot with a built-in water reservoir, add a moisture sensor and a small pump, and reduce your maintenance to four or five fill-ups a year. Other imaginative people have hacked old coffee machines to drip-feed their plants. It's fun, but it's just one way to grow houseplants. If you're an old-school plant parent and do it all on analog tech, that's fine!

SETTING YOUR GOALS AND CREATING YOUR ROUTINE

Unlike the previous chapter-end quizzes, this one doesn't add up your answers at the end to deliver a verdict. It's just here as a way for you to think through your first few seasons as a plant parent. So take your time assessing the options rather than rushing through to tick all the boxes.

In the next chapter, we'll take a look at the nitty gritty of plant maintenance on a daily basis, so you can start achieving your goals.

QUIZ

1. Why do you want houseplants?
   a) They're pretty.
   b) I miss being able to get out into nature.
   c) I'm fascinated by plants, or by a particular species of plant.
   d) I want something to look after.
2. Which of these would make a good short-term goal for you?
   a) Have five thriving plants by the end of the year.
   b) Focus on different varieties of the same plant.
   c) Get my top three herbs to grow on my kitchen windowsill.
   d) Build a small indoor garden of succulents.
3. Which of these could be a long-term goal for you?
   a) Have just the right plants in my home and know I can look after them.
   b) Grow some really challenging ferns and orchids.
   c) Learn how to propagate the plants I grow.
   d) Become an expert on cacti and maybe even go to see some in the wild.
   e) Enjoy teaching my kids how to grow microgreens.
4. How do you feel about automated plant maintenance?
   a) I could really get into programming some detailed instructions for each of my plants.
   b) It's useful if I'm going to be away for a while.
   c) I don't trust a machine to look after my babies.
   d) It's a bit too much work setting it all up.
5. What's the best way to remember your plant care schedule?
   a) Write it down and stick it up with a fridge magnet.
   b) Get my smartphone to remind me.
   c) Always do it first thing in the morning.
   d) Get my smartphone to remind my butler/BFF/mom.

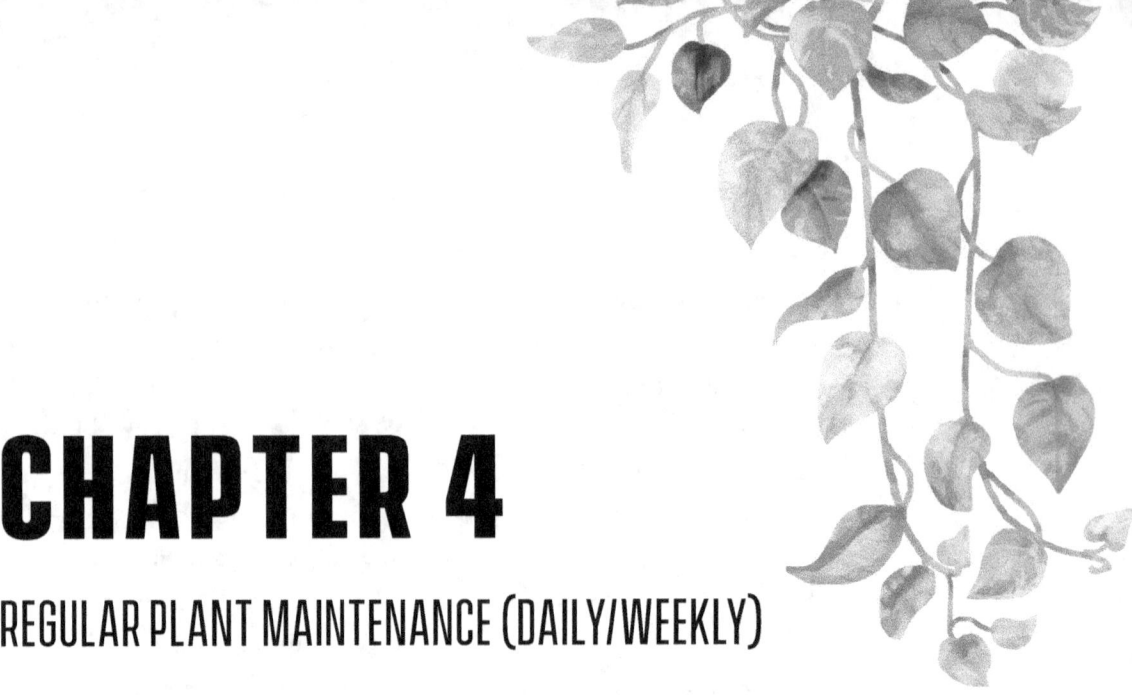

CHAPTER 4
REGULAR PLANT MAINTENANCE (DAILY/WEEKLY)

Interior design expert and TV host Bobby Berk knows all about what makes a house into a home, and he reckons plants have a lot to do with it. "A plant is the most cliché thing," he says, "but a little bit of green has a great effect on happiness. Being in a cubicle all day is not pleasing, but a little life on your desk can give you a little life, too."

But living with plants means caring for plants, and particularly if you're a city person through and through, it's not always easy to know what they need. This is where a lot of people go wrong. "My plants need water," they say, and water their poor babies to death. Or "I need to put my plant somewhere nice and bright," and the next thing they know, all the leaves have gone brown and begun to die because the plant doesn't like direct sunlight.

So this chapter is about the practicalities of daily and weekly plant care. We started to talk about this in the last chapter but we are going to delve much deeper. Hopefully it will give you answers to all your basic anxieties, like "How much water is too much?" and "How do I know if my plant is happy or not?" And it will explain how to create a really simple, basic routine that will keep your plants healthy and keep you happy and stress-free.

 ## WATER WISDOM

The one thing you need to remember is always to water when it's needed, not because the schedule tells you to. 'When it's needed' will depend on the individual plant and its preferences, but it actually isn't that difficult to tell, as long as you remember which plants like moist soil and which ones like to dry out before they get another drink.

Water in the morning, if you can (it's less important for houseplants than it is for outdoor plants, but it's still good practice). For plants in really warm, south-facing windows, make sure you water before the sun gets hot, so the water sinks in and doesn't evaporate.

Giving a really good watering less frequently is usually better for plants than dribbling a little bit of water into the pot on a daily basis. Keep pouring till the soil is really soaked, and you see water running out of the bottom of the pot. Check back in a quarter of an hour to dump any water that's run into the saucer, so that the plant doesn't get waterlogged; or water your plants in the sink and put them back on their saucers once there's no more water draining out.

Some plants, particularly succulents, want to be watered from the bottom; put them in the sink and let them soak water up. This keeps the water off the fragile foliage, and also helps to develop the plant's root system.

Avoid waterlogging. Never leave water in the saucer or planter.

Water needs to reach the roots of the plant, not its leaves. Water evenly around the plant, keeping the leaves and stem dry. Even with plants that like humidity, getting water on the leaves lets it run down and pool in crevices where it can lead to rot. Don't let the water just pool on the surface of the soil; make sure it is running all the way through.

Root growth can be assisted by letting plants dry out slightly before the next watering, even if they're the kind that like moister soil. As the plant finds less moisture close by, it will send its roots out a little further to see if it can find more. Over time, that can help your plant create a healthy and strong root ball. For plants which like to dry out between waterings, ensure the soil has really dried out all the way through, using your finger or a moisture meter to test.

Understand seasonality: plants often want less water in winter, when they're not growing or may even be dormant.

Make your life easier by grouping plants with similar watering needs together – cacti and succulents in one place, ferns and orchids in another. Or color-code your plants – red for 'let me dry out first,' green for 'keep my soil moist.'

Check your plants daily. *Water* them when they need it.

Checking in with your plants first thing can actually be a joyful morning ritual – your chance to touch nature before you turn on the computer or grab the car keys.

HOW DO YOU KNOW THE PLANT IS THIRSTY?

When you're checking your plants, feel the soil with your finger. Don't just feel the top part of the soil; push your finger right in up to the second joint, particularly if the pot is a big one. If the soil is totally dry, with not a trace of moisture, then your plant needs water. If your finger comes out without any soil sticking to it, that's pretty dry (you can also check by using the kind of chopsticks that come with sushi or Chinese takeaway; if the chopstick comes out without any soil stuck to it, there's no moisture left in the soil).

When you've done this, remember to fill the hole up, and try not to compact the soil.

Another way to check, particularly for cacti and succulents, is to use pebbles to landscape the pot; pick up one of the pebbles and you can easily see if there's any moisture on the underside, as it will be darker than the top of the stone. If it's still moist, you don't need to water just yet.

For really small pots just do a pinch test: rub the soil between finger and thumb. If it's dry, add a little water, but remember there could still be moisture beneath, so don't over-water. The reason you're not going to do a full finger-probe for a plant in a tiny pot is that you probably will disturb the roots, so it's better not to run that risk.

Or of course you can use a moisture probe (discussed in Chapter 3). It's more exact than the finger test, and even if you prefer to use your finger, using the probe can help train you to detect moisture more accurately. If you like, you're using it to calibrate your fingers. A probe can also go further down the pot, and you may find that while the top has dried out, there's still moisture further down a large pot.

And remember, the above is general watering advice. Always check the requirements of a particular plant to see when it likes to be watered; some plants for example like to have their soil kept moist all of the time. See the Appendix in the back of the book which details specific watering needs for fifty common houseplants.

HOW DO YOU KNOW THE PLANT IS WATERLOGGED?

A number of things can happen when a plant's pot is waterlogged. Its leaves may start yellowing, go soft or squishy, or start getting brown edges. It may start losing its leaves. The stem could start to go squishy, and the soil might smell bad. You may also see little flies around the bottom of the stem.

Your first test is to stick a finger in the pot. If it's waterlogged, you'll be able to tell very easily, and then you will need to check the roots for root rot. Lay down some paper or a bin bag to keep the mess contained, and pull the plant gently out of the pot. Expose the roots and take a good look. Healthy roots are white in color and firm in texture; rotting roots are brown and squishy.

If all the roots have rotted, your plant is beyond saving. Wrap the soil and the plant up and put it in the trash can, then clean up your hands and any tools you used, and put the pot in diluted bleach for a while.

If only some of the roots have rotted, then trim off the brown roots, leaving the clean white roots attached to the plant. Knock as much soil as possible off the clean roots, and then throw away the infected soil as well as the dead roots. Use a fungicide on the plant. You may want to prune the foliage back if the root pruning has been severe. Use fresh soil to repot the plant.

FINGER TEST

HOW DO YOU KNOW THE PLANT ISN'T GETTING ENOUGH WATER?

A plant that isn't getting enough water may have leaves that become droopy or flat. Its leaves may wilt – the classic sign of under-watering – and the tips of the leaves may become brown, then the edges. Leaf drop can be a sign of over-watering or of under-watering; of course, checking the soil in the pot will tell you which is the case.

Sometimes you can see that the soil is pulling away from the sides of the pot. This means that the soil has become compacted, and you need to rehydrate by soaking the whole pot for a few minutes to fully moisten the soil. Putting the pot in the sink and letting it soak up water is probably the best way to help a plant that hasn't had enough water, rather than just watering with the watering can, but remember to let the pot drain out again before you put the plant in its saucer.

CONSISTENCY

You do need to be consistent in your routines. This is one of those things that many beginners don't appreciate; they think they will just know when a plant needs water. You need to check consistently. It can also be useful, when you start with a new plant, to record how much water it wanted each time. Every plant is different, even within species, so having a month's worth of records to look back on gives you an idea how much that plant usually needs – two full waterings a week, or only every third time you checked.

(It's also useful to keep records of other interventions, such as feeding and pruning. You'll get to know how often particular plants need trimming back, or how much fertilizer got them to perk up, and that's a good guide for the future. You can even use these data to build reminders into your calendar for when the plant will probably next need attention).

What you *shouldn't* do is have a 'watering schedule.' Imagine if someone told you that at seven in the evening, every day, you would be given the same meal, whether you were hungry or not, whatever you'd eaten at lunchtime, because that was a good schedule. If you have a schedule for watering, and don't check the pot first, that's basically what you're doing to your plants.

So your routine is as follows: every day at whatever time, check the pots, with your watering can in your hand, and if any of your plants really need watering, give them some water (if all your plants are succulents, cacti, or other plants that prefer the soil to dry out between waterings, then you might make your checks bi-weekly. Succulents may only need watering every three weeks). A more pleasing way to think of this schedule is: "Let's go for a mindful morning stroll through our indoor forest."

WHAT WATER SHOULD YOU USE?

This is not a silly question! Water is basically H_2O, but of course it may contain all kinds of other elements. Your tap water might be chlorinated, fluoridated, or softened, and this can affect its suitability for watering your plants.

Tap water is *usually* okay, but if you have a way to collect rainwater, that is better for your plants; chlorine often has a bad effect. You can also let tap water sit for twenty-four hours before using it, or boil it for fifteen minutes. This will reduce the chlorine levels. You can also use a charcoal-based water filter, like the kind of filter you use with a water filtration jug.

Don't use softened water for your plants. Sodium carbonate is used for water softening and means there's too much salt in the water for plants to take.

If you have a fish tank, aquarium water is great for your plants. You need to change it every so often, so put the old water in your watering can. It will be full of nutrients.

If you have softened, highly chlorinated water, no fish tank and no way of collecting rainwater, then you will end up having to use mineral water but that can get expensive and is environmentally damaging (at least try to make sure the bottles are made from recycled plastic). You could also get a home filter.

Remember that plants are living things and have different water needs at different times or in different circumstances. There are a lot of factors that can affect how much water a plant needs, for instance:

HOW MUCH WATER DOES A PLANT NEED?

- Young plants are still developing their root systems, and dry out quickly, so they will tend to need more frequent watering. Older plants have more efficient roots which can find water deeper in the pot, so they can go longer between waterings.
- When it is particularly hot or dry, plants will need more water.
- Plants that are growing strongly will need more water than those that are slow growers.
- Plants in spring may need more water as they wake up – in winter, when they're dormant or less active, they'll need less.

By the way, remember when you are potting your plants to make sure that the soil is right for the plant – some will prefer quick draining soil, others prefer a moister mix. If you get the soil right, you're minimizing the likelihood of watering problems.

LIGHT AND TEMPERATURE CONTROL

If you already put your houseplants in the right light, and your home is adequately heated, then that's half your work done. But just as with watering, you'll want to check that your plants are happy with the amount of light and warmth they're getting.

Plants will usually give you signs that they are getting too much or too little light. Scorched or bleached leaves show they're getting too much light, or direct light rather than their preferred indirect light. Pale or yellowing leaves show that they are not producing chlorophyll (green pigment) because they're not getting enough light. 'Leggy' stems, large spaces between leaf nodes, plants that are 'stretching' towards the light, and failure to flower can also be signs of lower light levels than the plant needs. Leaf drop might be another symptom, and many variegated or colored plants start to revert towards green if they don't receive enough light.

Don't trust your eyes; trust your light meter. Our eyes automatically adjust to different light levels, and we are not good judges. Plants are usually more accurate than we are in knowing how much light is enough.

How can you help your plants get the right amount of light? Repositioning them can help; sometimes you just need to move a plant closer to or further away from the window. Or you can throw a little shade, using a muslin curtain, or a bigger plant, or even a box of cereal, to shade the plant from direct sunlight.

You can add artificial lighting; this can also help a plant into flower, if the spring where you are is not quite coming through with enough strong daylight to wake up your houseplants. We talk about this in more detail later in the book.

With artificial lighting, it's important to remember that plants still need a regular day/night cycle. Any electrical timer can help you provide this automatically because, let's face it, we all have better things to do than spend half an hour before we go to sleep switching off all the plant lights.

KEEPING THE RIGHT TEMPERATURE

Remember to check the temperature when you're walking round your internal garden. You need to check how warm it is right where the plant is, not just on the thermostat in the hall, as temperature varies depending on how far the plant is from radiators, whether there are any drafts, the presence of uninsulated walls or single glazed windows, and so on.

Be aware of when the heating comes on; if you put plants near radiators, they could cook! Likewise, in summer, if the air con comes on automatically, remember the needs of your plants and stop the temperature falling below their comfort level. It's surprisingly easy to forget that our heating and ventilation systems might work without our noticing it.

If you can, try to dial the heating down a little for the night. If plants experience a night-time temperature 10F or 5C lower than the daytime temperature, it helps them keep a regular daily rhythm, which will keep them healthy.

Remember that window panes can be cold in winter, so make sure in the fall that your plants' leaves are kept well away from the window pane. If you need to, move the plants back to keep them warm.

HUMIDITY CONTROL

Some plants may want humidity without needing more water; they want humidity in the air, not round their roots. Air plants, for instance, don't even put their roots in soil, so they get all their moisture from air. If you find that a plant's leaves are yellowing, or flower buds are falling off, but the pot is not dry, it's quite likely that low humidity is the issue.

Putting a humidifier in the room is by far the best way to increase the humidity. A mister won't have so much impact, though if you group plants together, they're more likely to benefit, as the vegetation will tend to retain humid air. A pebble tray – a tray filled with pebbles, and with water dribbled under the pebbles – can also help, as the water should slowly evaporate. It's important not to let the water get so high in the tray that it's sucked up into the pot's drainage hole. As with a humidifier, grouping plants on a pebble tray will further assist in keeping the right humidity levels.

PLANT ON PEBBLE TRAY

ROTATING PLANTS

Plants will always grow towards the light. In the open, they get light on all sides, so this doesn't happen so often in nature; in your house, they may only get light from one side, and so they'll lean towards it. That may end up making them look very odd, and worse, they may not grow many leaves on the 'back' side, so they will look bare.

To stop this happening, you need to rotate the plant on a regular basis; this is one case where you want a super-consistent schedule. Don't wait till a plant starts to lean, then give it a dramatic change; rotate it a little bit every so often. That lets it get used to the change without undue stress.

Fast-growing plants in bright light should get a quarter turn every month; slower growing plants in medium or low light should get a weekly rotation, but of just 45 degrees. It doesn't matter which direction you turn the plant, as long as you're consistent; don't turn it clockwise one time, then anti-clockwise the next. I always forget which way to go, so I have marked all my pots with a hidden arrow in marker pen to show me what to do.

If you have really big and heavy pots, put them on a wheeled pot base or a lazy Susan so they are easy to rotate.

ACTIVITY: MAKE LABELS FOR YOUR PLANTS

One way to remember exactly what each plant likes is to make a customized label with all the information on it.

Create a template with headings for watering, temperature, light, compost type, and other information (e.g. 'needs pruning every month' or 'feed with tomato fertilizer'). Why not spend a little time thinking of neat symbols for some of the information rather than just writing it down in words? That can make the label much easier to read.

Now, for each of your plants, look at the advice in chapter three and at your plant's label (if it came from a shop or nursery) and summarize its needs.

If you computerize your labels, you can always print another one out when the old one gets tatty. I like to get mine laminated so water doesn't get in and they are stiff enough to poke into the pot. On the other hand, a friend uses lollipop sticks color-coded with electrical tape – green for 'moist earth,' yellow for 'dry out between waterings' and red for 'arid' – and with notches for light levels. Another (geeky) friend has QR codes on the pots that link to an entire page on the plant.

What works for you?

Make a Difference with Your Review
Houseplant Care Made Easy

"Plants can't buy happiness, but caring for them can." *Anonymous*

People who give without expecting anything back live longer, happier lives. So if we can do that during our time together, let's give it a try.

To make that happen, I have a question for you...

Would you help someone you've never met, even if you never got credit for it?

Who is this person, you ask? They are like you. Or, at least, like you used to be. Less experienced, wanting to make a difference, and needing help, but not sure where to look.

My mission is to make houseplant care accessible to everyone. And, the only way for me to accomplish that mission is by reaching...well...everyone.

This is where you come in. Most people do, in fact, judge a book by its cover (and its reviews). So here's my ask on behalf of a struggling plant lover you've never met:

Please help that plant lover by leaving this book a review.

Your gift costs no money and less than 60 seconds to make real, but can change a fellow plant lover's life forever. Your review could help...

- Another small business thrive in the plant community.
- A plant shop employee find meaningful work.
- A reader transform their living space.
- A dream of a green oasis come true

To get that 'feel good' feeling and help this person for real, all you have to do is leave a review and it takes less than 60 seconds.

Simply scan the QR code below to leave your review (just so you know, this takes you to the review page of Amazon US, if you live in a different country, simply change the .com to the relevant country domain suffix. Or you can go to your order page to leave a review there):

I'm excited to help you achieve happy, healthy houseplants faster and easier than you can possibly imagine. You'll love the tips and tricks I'm about to share in the coming chapters.

Thank you from the bottom of my heart. Now, back to our regularly scheduled program.

Your biggest fan, Nydia Needham

PS - Fun fact: If you provide something of value to another person, it makes you more valuable to them. If you believe this book will help another plant lover, send it their way.

CHAPTER 5

REGULAR PLANT MAINTENANCE (MONTHLY/YEARLY)

Humorist, storyteller and photographer David Hobson has built a marvelous garden in Waterloo, Ontario, Canada – and a huge collection of houseplants. What's his motivation? "I grow plants for many reasons," he says "to please my eye or to please my soul, to challenge the elements or to challenge my patience, for novelty or for nostalgia, but mostly for the joy in seeing them grow."

That joy in seeing them grow isn't something that will happen overnight. It's something that will catch you by surprise one day when you realize that spindly little plant you brought home has begun to fill out and spread, or after a year and a half you finally see a tiny flower bud appear on that lonely cactus. It's a joy that will last over the long term. And it means that you're also going to need to think about some long-term maintenance, things you don't need to do every day but maybe every couple of months or just once a year. In some cases, even every two or three years!

That's what this chapter's about.

 ## FEEDING

Although plants get their energy from photosynthesis – turning light into energy – they also need various minerals to thrive. That means they'll need feeding from time to time, to give them a boost. While potting compost includes the nutrients they need, most plants will have used those nutrients up within a couple of months, so they'll need regular replenishment. The three basic nutrients are nitrogen, potassium, and phosphorous, but different plants will need different mixes of the three, and some also need other elements such as magnesium or calcium. Think of fertilizer as a plant's multivitamin supplement.

You can use general fertilizers, but you should dilute them to half or quarter strength, as houseplants are slower growing and don't need as much as plants growing outside. Or you can use fertilizer made specially for houseplants; even then, some plants which are very light feeders will want to have it diluted heavily. Some plants have very specific needs; cacti need low-nitrogen fertilizer, and you'll find fertilizer specially made for cacti and succulents at most good gardening stores. Plants which flower need fertilizer with a little more phosphorous in (the Appendix in the back of the book includes the fertilizing needs of fifty of the most common houseplants).

The dosage and frequency depends on both the kind of fertilizer you use, and the needs of each specific plant. Most succulents don't need so much, and orchids do better with less rather than too much. Fertilizer requirements will also tend to be seasonal; plants don't need much fertilizer in the winter. You want to start feeding them again once they wake up in spring.

Read the label for directions on how often you need to feed a plant. The hungriest plants like to be fed every couple of weeks, but many others want monthly feeds, and cacti might only want a single feed every year. Rather than overfeed, which is basically an overdose for a plant, you will be safer giving plants a lower dosage slightly more often, so the plant can cope more easily with the high nutrient level.

Don't forget to keep a record of when you last fertilized each plant and build a reminder into your diary.

There are various types of fertilizer delivery: liquid fertilizers, sticks, powders (that are mixed into the surface of the soil) and granules. The big advantage of liquid fertilizer is that you can add it easily as part of your watering routine. Mixing granules and powders into the soil can be messy, though it does have the advantage of a slower release. If you want a slow-release fertilizer, the sticks are much less messy, and you have no danger of overdoing things by accident.

There are a few DIY options available as well. For instance, some people use dried coffee grounds, which contain nitrogen, phosphorous, potassium, and are slightly acidic. Snake plant and jade plant will love you for sharing your coffee with them, and apparently it will perk up Christmas cactus, too (remember to let the coffee grounds cool down first!) However, though this works for succulents growing outdoors, the jury is out on how well it works for houseplants in pots. All I know is it works for me.

Crushed eggshells introduce lime (containing calcium) to the soil, which is alkali, so that's good for plants that don't like acidic soil. Aloe vera, asparagus fern and geraniums all prefer alkaline soil. You could also add a little sifted wood ash, but it's easy to overdo it – eggshells are a better bet.

REPOTTING

One of the joys of watching your houseplants grow is seeing how quickly some of them outgrow the pot they first came in. That's not the only time you might want to repot a plant, though. Sometimes, a plant just needs new soil, in the same pot; changing the soil means the plant gets a boost of fresh nutrients.

Faster growing plants might need to be repotted every year, or even oftener; slower growing, or larger specimens, might only need repotting every eighteen months or two years.

Another time you'll need to repot is if the plant has had root rot or another disease; you'll want to change the soil, and make sure you throw out the old soil to avoid cross-contamination.

If you're repotting because a plant has grown, then you need to be careful to get just the right size of new pot. You don't want it to be more than two to four inches wider than it is already. It's like buying clothes for children, you don't buy a two-year-old clothes they'll only grow into by the time they're six, you buy them clothes with just a little extra growing space. If the new pot is too large, it won't just look weird, but the extra soil will retain too much water for the plant's needs.

How do you tell when a plant really needs repotting? There are quite a few clear signs:

- The roots are growing out of the drainage hole.
- The roots are pushing the plant up above the surface of the soil.
- The plant has stopped growing.
- The plant is three times the size of its planter (looking at the mass of the foliage, not the height of the plant).
- The potting mix dries out too quickly, and much more quickly than it used to.
- You can see salt build-up on the pot or on the surface of the soil.

You may want to keep a record of which plants are close to needing repotting, then do them all at once. Choose a good time, while the plants are dormant, or just before spring arrives.

REPOTTING A HOUSE PLANT

HOW TO REPOT YOUR PLANTS

What you'll need:

- Potting tarp or a bin liner.
- Watering can.
- Gardening gloves.
- Diluted bleach.
- Potting mix.

Your first job is to clear a space on a table or at the sink and lay down a potting tarp or a bin bag liner to catch all the loose soil. If you're not repotting at the sink, have your watering can or a bottle of water at the ready. If you're repotting cacti, other prickly plants, or toxic plants (like ficus species and euphorbias, which have sap that can irritate your skin) then wear a good, stout pair of gardening gloves. At this point, if you have new pots for your plants, you should clean them with a little diluted bleach (yes, even if they came straight from a store). They're ready to use and you won't have to stop halfway through repotting to clean them (don't ask me how I know that).

Lie the plant down sideways to remove it gently from the pot. You can be much more gentle this way than trying to lift it up into the air with the pot on the table. If it's proving difficult to move, tap the bottom of the pot; you might also need to use a knife or spatula to scrape the soil away from the sides of the pot.

Once the plant is out, put the pot aside for cleaning. Loosen the roots of the plant gently. If the plant is root-bound, you'll see the roots winding round and round tightly, you need to try to loosen them, and maybe even give them a trim. When you prune roots, don't prune the thicker parts, just the thin, threadlike roots inbetween them. That way, you leave the main structure intact and the plant can start growing again from there.

Remove the old potting mix and throw it out. The soil is completely exhausted. If you have a garden or a municipal compost facility, that's where it goes – better in the municipal compost, which gets nice and hot and will kill off any diseases, should there be any.

If you are reusing the same pot, you now need to clean it with diluted bleach. If you're using a new pot, it should be ready. Add new potting mix about a third of the way up the pot. Now put the plant in the pot to test if the level is about right. The soil level needs to come to the same place on the stem that it did in the old pot, so you might want to add a bit more compost or take a bit out to fit the plant well to the new pot.

Once you've got that right, put the plant in the pot, resting it on the compost that's already there, and hold it while you pour new potting mix around it. Press the potting mix down a little, but not too hard; the plant should be secure but the soil should be open enough that the roots have room to breathe.

Now give the plant a really good watering, until the water comes out of the bottom of the pot, and let it drain in the sink or into a bowl til there is no more water running out. Now it's ready to put in its planter or on its saucer. This watering will give the plant a boost so that it can recover from all the excitement.

Your plant won't need any fertilizer for the next six to eight weeks, because there are nutrients in the new soil that it has to use up first. It may sulk for a bit, but after a month or so you should see it starting to grow again.

 ## PRUNING, CLEANING, GROOMING

Keeping your houseplants healthy is the first part of being a good plant parent but you'll also want to make sure that they look their best. Primping your plants is just an extra layer on top of your regular plant care routine.

You may be looking at a jade plant, for instance, and realize that one of its branches has grown way too long, and the plant looks unbalanced. So if you want your plant to be symmetrical, you'll want to just prune that branch back to make the plant shapely again. Or you might just take off the tip of a branch; that will stop it continuing to grow straight up, and make it branch out instead.

Or you might see a leaf that is dying, somewhere toward the base of a plant. Old leaves do die, that's perfectly normal, but if you leave them there they can look nasty and also expose the plant to various kinds of diseases. So don't wait til it falls off: just remove it neatly.

Pinching is the first way to take off leaves and small branches. Make sure your hands are clean, then just use your thumb and finger to pinch off the tip of a stem or a leaf. Pinching off the growing tips helps stop a plant growing too high too fast and can help to keep a plant bushy instead of letting it sprawl. Always pinch just above a leaf node, the little bump where a leaf is attached.

Pinching off the growing tips is particularly important for basil, mint and sage. If you let the plants flower, they won't put any more effort into growing those nice leaves for your kitchen.

You can also cut a stem with sharp scissors. Cut above a leaf node, and cut at a 45-degree angle, not straight across; this stops water pooling, and avoids disease. Make sure your scissors are really sharp, and don't pull on the stems or leaves. You need to make good clean cuts, since tears and ragged cuts can give an opening to fungal diseases. You should also remember to wash your scissors, or wipe them with antibacterial wipes, in between each plant, to avoid any possibility of contamination.

Pruning houseplants is best done in the growth season, in spring or summer (that's different from some outdoor plants which are pruned when dormant). However, getting rid of dying leaves and pinching out tips can be done at any time.

If you grow flowering houseplants, dead-heading is important. First of all, you don't want to have ugly fading and dead flowers in view; that's depressing. More important for the plant, the dead flowers might start rotting and encourage mold; and also, they waste the plant's energy. Many plants will not produce more flowers unless you remove the dead ones; if you do your dead-heading properly, you'll keep the plant blooming for far longer than it would naturally.

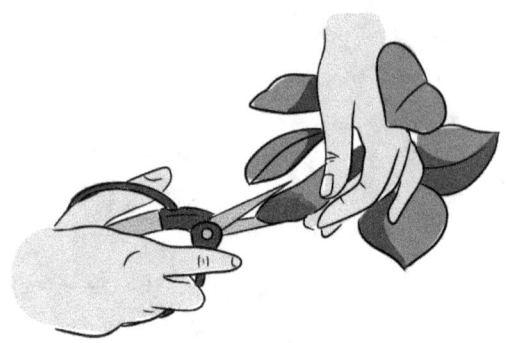

PRUNING A HOUSE PLANT

SPECIFIC TIPS

There are a couple of special cases here. If you want to save seeds, you won't want to deadhead the plant; leave the flowers on it and the seeds and seedcase will eventually develop. And if you want fruit from a citrus tree, leave the flowers undisturbed.

Flowering can be a big drain on a plant's energy, so in the case of very young plants which are still getting established, de-budding might be advisable. Just pinch off the flower buds and the plant will be able to redirect its energy to growing its root system and its leaves. Then it will be in much better shape to flower next year.

Pruning is something of an art. When a branch is dead, or growing the wrong way, you can take the whole branch off. You might need to prune a plant that is becoming spindly and leggy, to force it to regrow in a more bushy way. You might need to prune it if for some reason it has grown unbalanced, or simply if it has grown much too big and is taking over your space. For foliage plants, prune at the beginning of the growing season; for flowering plants, though, a good time to prune is just after flowering.

Don't just take your scissors and get started. Before you do any cutting, take a good look at the plant. It can help if you put it on a table and walk around it. Where is it growing? Where is it not growing? How does its structure compare with the way it should look? How does its size compare with the space you have for it? Are there any bare patches? Are there places where it looks as if it isn't getting any air, because the branches have grown too closely together?

Move on to thinking about where to cut in order to address the problems you've spotted. Then, and only then, it's time to pick up the scissors and make your first cut. You can remove up to a quarter of the plant without any ill effects.

If the plant is looking a bit leggy and bare, and you want it to grow back more bushy, stagger your cuts. Snip off just the tips on some branches, and cut others back by a quarter, a half, or even all the way to the stem. It will grow back and branch from where you cut it, filling up the center nicely. Remember to take out any dead stems or branches.

There are just a few plants that you should never prune: palms, Norfolk Island pines, and orchids (with orchids, just remove the dead flower spikes).

Plants that grow outside get cleaned by the wind and rain. With houseplants, you'll need to clean them yourself. You want to keep them looking good, but cleaning them regularly also helps keep pests away, and helps the plant get as much light as possible. If the leaves are dusty, the plant isn't going to get all the light it could.

Plants with big smooth leaves like monstera or banana will want to be wiped clean with a cloth or sponge that's damp (not wet). Don't use the same cloth/sponge on another plant without cleaning it first. Hairy-leaved plants can be dusted down with a soft brush like an artist's paintbrush or a makeup brush; don't use any water when you're doing this. Ferns, on the other hand, actually like a good shower – spray them gently with water, or even take them outside in summer to give them a good spray and let them dry off in the sun before they come back in.

 ## KEEPING A PLANT JOURNAL

Keeping a plant journal is a great way to keep track of your plants' growth. You don't need to write down every time that you water the plant or trim off a dead leaf or two, but it can be really useful when you have a 10-foot plant and want to know how big it was when you bought it, or when you can't remember last time your prize monstera was repotted.

If you customize your journal with photos or drawings, it can become a source of joy and pride that you can look at to remember how you started and how far you've come. You might want a functional style journal with reminders of important dates, and a calendar to keep track, or a journal a bit more like a 'baby book' that records your plant's growth.

Think about the actions you want to track and how you want to track them. For example, you might want to track watering, if you're interested in learning just how much a particular variety needs. You might give each plant four pages – one with photos, one with drawings, one with dates of pruning and 'before' and 'after' photos, and one with dates of watering, feeding and repotting. You might want to use a ready-made journal or a loose-leaf binder. You might even want to do the whole thing on a database or on your smartphone.

Most importantly, you want to write in *what works for your plant*. "I gave him an extra-hard pruning, and he shot up by six inches in a month!" or "Adding an extra glow-light got this plant flowering two weeks earlier this year." You can also write in what doesn't work, but try not to fixate on it!

Don't forget to write up your journal at least once a week, or daily if you can. It will be a fantastic resource for you in future.

You've got the basics now, and you're ready to go buy some houseplants. If you're still worried about your ability to care for your plant babies, you'll love the next chapter; we'll take a look at the toughest plants around, the ones you can mistreat, over-water, neglect, and they'll *still* keep growing. These are the ones you practically can't kill.

CHAPTER 6

THE TOUGHEST PLANTS AROUND

What do the dandelion, stinging nettle, couch grass, and ivy all have in common?

You might answer, "They're all weeds." But as Winnie-the-Pooh creator A.A.Milne once said, "Weeds are flowers too, once you get to know them." And in fact, these plants are weeds because they are really tough little critters, fast to grow, not picky or choosy about where they grow, and very difficult to kill. If you're just starting out as a plant parent, the houseplants you want have a lot in common with weeds!

To misquote the poet Elizabeth Barrett Browning: "How shall I kill thee? Let me count the ways." I have managed to kill plants in all these ways:

- Forgetting to bring in a plant I'd put outside to catch the sun. Of course, that was the only night that month that we got frost.
- Repotting a plant into a pot that didn't have a drainage hole in the bottom. The poor thing ended up sinking into a muddy swamp.
- Putting cacti on a shelf in the bathroom. You guessed it: cacti don't like humidity, and they like bright light. That was not my smartest move.
- Believing the word 'easy' when the local garden center had air plants. They looked great for a while. Then… they didn't.
- Forgetting when we had a heatwave to take my herbs off the kitchen windowsill where the sun was beating in. They frizzled (I like them cooked, but I tend to chop them up first).

- The orchid in a lovely china pot. Actually, I blame that one on my cat. I found the orchid on the floor one day surrounded by smashed bits of china, and the orchid never really recovered. Moral: don't put small, light pots where your cat can get at them.
- Over-watering. And then over-watering the same plant even more, because the plant looked like it was dying.
- I finally decided to borrow a sophisticated watering system from my geeky friend so I could go on holiday without worrying. Of course… I forgot to switch it on.

Yes, that's right, you have bought a book about houseplants from a mass houseplant murderer. Which is a good thing, because if I can make all those mistakes and still, eventually, learn to keep happy healthy houseplants, so can you.

And a big step in my progress was when I found some really indestructible plants to get started with. I call them "The Invincibles." Some plants are quite easy to cope with but if you get it wrong, they will die. Other plants will tolerate just about anything you can throw at them.

SO, WHAT ARE WE LOOKING FOR IN AN INVINCIBLE?

- It needs to be a resilient plant — usually that also means it's a fast grower.
- It needs to be able to adapt to different levels of light and humidity.
- It should be able to survive neglect if you don't water it for while.
- It should be low maintenance and easy to look after. It might not look its best without TLC, but it won't die.
- It's also really helpful if it's an air purifying plant that will do you some good.

I also like it if Invincibles are easy to propagate. That means I'll always have baby plants, so I always have "an heir and a spare," like the British royal family!

WHICH PLANTS ARE INVINCIBLE?

PONYTAIL PALM

The ponytail palm is one of the Invincibles. In fact, it's a kind of agave even though it looks more like a palm tree. You can forget to water it, and it mainly won't care. It might scorch if it's in direct sunlight, but it won't die. It doesn't care whether your house is dry or a bit more humid. The only way you can kill it is to chuck it in a tub of water, really.

And ponytails will grow to a great age. They can last twenty years with very little maintenance.

ZZ PLANT

ZZ PLANT

The ZZ plant is another Invincible. Again, they'll live for decades. It's not choosy about light conditions, you can even put it in quite a dim room; it's not choosy about humidity, either. It can go two, three or even four weeks without watering, as a bit like a camel stores water in its hump, it stores water in its thick stem. And it will grow really impressive with age. You might even get ZZ babies.

GOLDEN POTHOS

Golden Pothos and some of the other varieties, like 'Marble Queen', are other Invincibles. They grow like nobody's business, and they're very forgiving. You can give them a good hard prune if you need to, and the haircut will just stimulate them to keep growing. In fact, if a pothos sulks, trim it back, and it will probably stop sulking! They grow in most light conditions (though the leaves will be prettier with higher light levels) and aren't dependent on high humidity. They can survive being forgotten for a week or so, if you forget to water them, though perhaps they're not quite as good as outlasting a drought as the wonderful ZZ plant.

SNAKE PLANT

Snake plant (Draecena trifasciata) is an Invincible and more. It comes in numerous varieties, though not all of them have the special Kryptonite genes; stick to the regular 'Laurentii' variety, though, and you have a superplant that is pretty much indestructible. It can tolerate low light, and it stores water in its leaves so that if you don't water it for a while, nothing drastic is going to happen.

It's probably my favorite Invincible, because it comes in a number of different species (about seventy in all) and colors, so once you've got used to looking after the regular plant, you can try some of the varieties. For instance, the whale fin plant (Dracaena masoniana) is a beauty with its huge, fin-shaped leaves, though it's a very slow grower. Cylindrica, as its name suggests, has cylindrical leaves which can make an intensely dramatic accent in a snake plant collection, and the 'Boncel' variety grows like a fan or a starfish. There are tall thin snake plants and short fat ones, variegated snake plants and solid green ones.

Even better, snake plants are really, really easy to propagate. You can divide them up into separate little plants and pot them on, you can cut a piece of the rhizome (root) and plant it in soil, or you can just tear off a leaf and stick it in some water – it will grow roots.

SPIDER PLANT

First snakes, then spiders! The spider plant is also next to impossible to kill. They don't like direct sunlight too much; their leaves will turn brown. And they don't like to be overwatered. But go on, just *try* killing one. They are really tough and will tolerate different conditions of light and humidity. You'll only manage to kill a spider plant if you keep its roots waterlogged all the time; and if you hang it up in a basket, which is one neat way to grow it, that will probably ensure you don't pour too much water in.

And again, the spider plant is easy to propagate. In fact, it will do the job itself, producing little baby spiders that hang down from the main plant and grow their own root system. Just cut the 'umbilical cord' and plant the babies in their own pots, and you have a whole load of new plants.

SPIDER PLANT

CHRISTMAS CACTUS

The Christmas cactus is beautifully easy to grow. In fact they can quickly outgrow their containers, so the biggest job you'll have is pruning and repotting. And they can sometimes be fussy with getting the right amount of sun and shade. If you prune after they've flowered, you'll save their strength for creating new stems, and get even more flowers next year. You can be pretty severe pruning and the plant will still survive. A plus point is that you can propagate new plants from the prunings very easily.

I know someone whose mother kept spider plants and Christmas cacti in the porch. They got direct sunlight, they roasted in summer and chilled in winter, they got watered once a week whether they needed it or not, and they never, ever got repotted, or got any feeding at all. They're still going strong after twenty years! If that level of neglect can't kill a plant, it's an Invincible.

PEACE LILY

The peace lily can be a tricky plant to get the best out of, but even though it has a bit of a temperament, it's a real survivor. Like most of these plants, if you really wanted to destroy it, the way to do it is to leave it sitting in a puddle of water. The nice thing, though, is that if it wants water, it will actually tell you: it's a bit of a drama queen, and will wilt and flop over, but it's not dying, it's just communicating. Give it a nice deep watering and it will be right as rain in no time.

It's incredibly rewarding, too, when you do get conditions just right – bright, indirect light and letting the potting mix dry out between waterings – and those huge white flowers with their yellow centers emerge from the glossy green leaves.

JADE PLANT

And finally, the whole *crassula* family are pretty easy to grow, but jade plant (Crassula ovata) is almost unkillable. Even people who can kill other plants have managed to keep jade plants alive. These plants will tolerate anything except being flooded out. They will tolerate a drought when you forget to water them, because they store water in their big, fleshy leaves. Though they like bright light, they will tolerate low light conditions; jade plant needs just four hours of light, which unless you live in the Arctic Circle is not likely to be an issue.

I have a jade plant that didn't get watered for three months. I just forgot. It wasn't where the other plants were in the living room, I'd put it on a shelf in the study and I just forgot it was there. It had dropped a few leaves to show me it was sulking, but it perked up as soon as I gave it a quick drench and since then it's just carried on growing. Perhaps it hopes to get so big that I *can't* forget it!

JADE PLANT

However, for those of you who have cats, dogs, or children, I should point out the downside of the Invincibles. They didn't get so tough by playing nice, and most of them are toxic if eaten. Either keep your toxic plants safely out of reach, or limit yourself to the safe options: spider plant, Christmas cactus, and ponytail palm.

The Invincibles will give you a trouble-free ride. But once you start adding other plants to your collection, you'll find that even if you do all the basics right, sometimes a plant can struggle, or sulk, or just fail to thrive. So in the next chapter, let's look at how you can tell when plant babies need some TLC, and what you can do to help them.

STEP 3
TROUBLESHOOTING AND EXPANDING

CHAPTER 7
COMMON PLANT PROBLEMS

Just like I did when I started, you've possibly already killed a plant or two. Don't be too hard on yourself. According to the website Garden Pals, the average millennial plant parent has already killed a total of *seven* houseplants. So if you've only managed to murder two, you're doing significantly better than average!

My worst, I think, was the plant I mentioned before; the one I over-watered. Then, because it was looking floppy and unhappy, I made things worse by giving it *more* water. Basically, I drowned it.

But that's an easy mistake to make if you don't know how to interpret what your plants are telling you. So this chapter is all about the kind of common problems you'll likely see, and how to spot them. Some plants will tell you loud and clear that there's something wrong; others, you'll have to check up on a bit more to see if they're doing okay.

 ## WATERING PROBLEMS

Let's start with watering, because that's the most common problem new plant parents face. We don't have an instinct for how much water a given plant needs. Even if you're a keen outside gardener, you may be way off base when you're watering houseplants. Remember, most houseplants come from tropical regions – most of your garden plants probably don't. Garden plants' roots can usually range freely, whereas your houseplants are stuck in a pot. And water can drain away into the deeper soil in the garden, whereas in a pot, it's going to stay there, ready to rot a plant's roots if it's too moist and humid.

Even if you have done your work and know that a plant likes a particular style of watering, for instance, it likes to be well watered but then dry out before you water it again, you can easily get things wrong. For instance, you might be interrupted by an urgent phone call and forget to drain the saucer after you've watered a plant, leaving it much wetter than it wants to be. So you should know the signs of over- and under-watering.

Be warned: sometimes the signs are ambiguous, and sometimes they might reflect other problems, such as light conditions that are too low, or low temperatures. Check the soil before you take any action!

OVER-WATERING

Signs of over-watering include:

- Yellowing leaves. This is the most common sign. At this point, with most plants, let them dry out and you'll be able to save them.
- Leaf drop, particularly when young leaves start dropping, not older ones. Again, if you catch this early, giving the right treatment you'll probably save the plant.
- Mold or mushrooms growing on top of the soil. If the soil is wet enough for a fungus, it's way too wet for houseplants. Let the soil dry out and scrape the mold off the top.
- Rotting stems. Sometimes you'll find a stem will actually pull out of the plant because it's rotted through.
- Edema – brown dots and bumps on the leaves of camellias or fiddle leaf figs, caused by excessive water pressure as the plant has drunk too much.
- Poor growth, particularly in a plant that was growing quite fast, is often a sign of over-watering.
- Little gnats around your plants. These little gnats are attracted by wet soil. Let the soil dry out and they'll disappear, but you might want to take off the top layer of soil and replace it (that's where they lay their eggs).
- Wilting leaves.
- Browning foliage.
- Smelly soil.

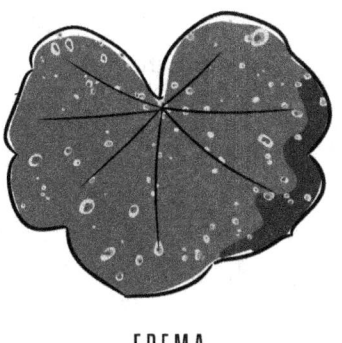
EDEMA

ROTTING STEMS

UNDER-WATERING

Signs of under-watering include:

- Wilting leaves, or leaves that are curling up on themselves.
- Droopy leaves.
- Browning foliage.
- The top surface of the soil has dried out.
- The pot feels crazily light when you pick it up.
- Slowing growth.
- New leaves are noticeably smaller than the old leaves.
- The soil is pulling away from the sides of the planter.
- Spider mites on the leaves of plants.

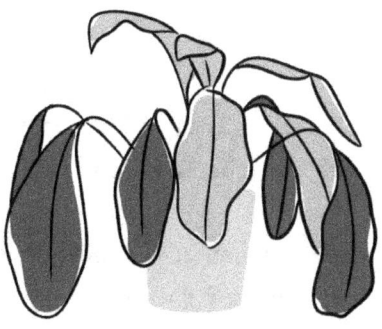
DROOPY LEAVES

Wilting leaves and browning foliage can be serious signs of either over- or under-watering! How can this be the case? The answer is that wilting might mean the plant isn't getting enough water from you. But it might also mean that the plant has root rot, because of continual over-watering, and that means although the soil is wet, the plant can't access the water through its roots, so it's become dehydrated.

To tell if a plant has root rot, you need to pull it out of its pot slightly, so that you can see the roots. Healthy roots should be white and quite strong. If they are brown or flabby, your plant has root rot. You'll need to trim the brown roots and leave just the healthy ones (if there are no healthy roots left, I'm sorry, but the plant has no chance).

It's easy, faced with wilting or browning, to find out which of these is the case. Poke your finger deep into the soil and it's easy to tell. If the soil is wet, you'll want to take the plant out of the pot and look at the roots. If the soil is dry, time for a watering!

HOW TO FIX WATERING PROBLEMS

Fix over-watering by letting the plant dry out thoroughly. If it's really wet, it's worth repotting the plant in dry soil and starting over. If the roots have started to rot, you need to cut out the rotted parts and prune the plant back (that was covered in Chapter four). It can take a few months for a plant to recover, so don't expect change overnight.

Under-watering is easier to fix; just give the plant a good soak. Some plants, like pothos, will recover in just a few hours; others take a bit longer. Recovery time also depends on how long the plant had been thirsty before you took action; it may take up to two weeks to replace foliage with new leaves if dehydration was advanced.

Remember to watch your plant carefully in the days after you take remedial action, so you can see if it has been overstressed.

If you have the same watering problem a few times, you'll want to take long term remedial action. You'll need to think about how you are treating your plants, and whether you need to change your routine.

For instance, over-watering might be happening because the temperature is headed down in the fall. Remember that plants need less water in winter; at the same time, water won't evaporate as fast, so regular watering could leave the plant wetter for longer than it did in summer.

You might want to assess whether your potting mix is draining fast enough. Adding some extra ingredients could improve the drainage; perlite, gravel, or even pumice are useful. Alternatively, your plant might be in a pot that is too big. If the roots don't take up more than a third of the space in the pot, the pot is too big and the plant can't drink up enough water to drain the soil. The result is that the soil outside the reach of the root ball will always be soaking. The answer here is to repot the plant in a smaller container.

Two other things should help you avoid over-watering: use porous pots, such as terracotta, and make sure your pots have drainage holes!

If under-watering is a regular problem, you might want to look and see if your plants have become root-bound. You might also want to assess whether your heating is part of the problem; if the temperature has gone up, or if central heating has reduced the humidity of your home.

You might also look at the way you're watering the plants. Are you soaking the soil properly or is water just running through the pot without being absorbed? Consider soaking the pots from the bottom, rather than using a watering can. The soil might also have become compacted on top, so a little addition of potting mix and some gentle scraping will help free it up.

Another contributor to under-watering could be a lack of organic material in the soil. Without enough organic matter, the soil won't retain water well. In this case a new potting mix, or the addition of perlite or vermiculite (which increase the soil's water retention) might be advisable.

If, on the other hand, you're simply forgetting to water your plants often enough, it's worth trying out watering globes or spikes, or even setting up an automatic system. Alternatively, and more cheaply, you could just get yourself more organized and set reminders in your phone!

Some plants might grow quite nicely in water rather than soil. That may sound counteractive as a way of solving over-watering. But waterlogging means that the water with its constituent oxygen is locked up in the soil and can't move; the plant can't get at it. It's this, not the fact that there's too much water, that is the real problem. If, on the other hand, you put a plant's roots directly in water, the water can move about, the circulation pulls in more oxygen from the air, and the plant can access the nutrients it needs.

Imagine, if you like, trying to drink through a water-soaked cloth. You wouldn't get enough water in your mouth. That's perhaps not the most scientific analogy, but that's the basic problem with waterlogging.

So for plants like lucky bamboo, philodendron, Chinese evergreen, spider plant, monstera, peace lily, cordyline, and many herbs, growing in water might work for you. But you'll still have to remember to feed them with nutrients from time to time, of course.

 ## FIXING LEGGY GROWTH

Lots of beginner houseplant parents find that after a while, they have problems with 'leggy' plants. When you were younger, did you know the kind of kid who suddenly shot up in height without filling out, becoming an uncoordinated, gangling beanpole who didn't know what to do with their arms and legs? Maybe you were one! A leggy plant is just like that.

Fortunately, it's not too difficult to rescue leggy plants and get them to look more attractive and properly filled out.

Increase the amount of light they are getting, through repositioning them or using a grow light. If the plant only gets light from one direction, rotation can help, but you might be better off putting it somewhere that it gets a wider source of light for a while, for instance, in a corner window.

Some plants, like hoyas and begonias, can become leggy if they don't have high enough humidity. A pebble tray or humidifier can help or, put them in the bathroom or kitchen for a while.

Pruning leggy plants can encourage them to grow back in a more compact form. Usually, if you pinch off the stem just above a leaf node, it will branch, rather than growing straight up again. One reason beginners so often end up with leggy plants is that they don't know how to do basic maintenance pruning, so plants get to run away with themselves.

 ## COMMON PLANT DISEASES

The signs of disease in houseplants are usually quite easy to see once you know what you're looking for. All kinds of blotches, fuzziness, leaf spots, cobwebby stuff, powder, and leaf deformations are suspicious.

COMMON DISEASES AND HOW TO TREAT THEM

White mold

White mold grows in fuzzy spots on the leaves of the plant. These mold spots aren't deadly; they like warm, dark and damp conditions, so one way to prevent them is to ensure your plants are well spaced to get the air. If you've got white mold or mildew, spray the plant with neem oil or a fungicide, or you could just wipe the plant down using dish soap with water, drying off the leaves afterwards.

Gray mold

Gray mold, or botrytis, is easy to spot. It tends to attack flowering plants such as African violets and cyclamen. If you cut off the dead leaves and flowers, you'll help to prevent it occurring. Like white mold, botrytis happens when the air doesn't circulate well enough around a plant, so a little pruning might be in order to open up the plant, or you might need to encourage a little more air circulation in your home. A fungicide or neem oil spray should clear gray mold up quickly.

Powdery mildew

Powdery mildew might look like white mold at first, but it's less fuzzy and more like cornstarch or talcum powder on the leaves. It won't kill plants, but it makes them weaker and can prevent them growing; it's also quite unsightly. Again, it's a sign of poor air circulation. Remember to tidy up fallen leaves and pinch off brown or dead leaves, as well as giving the plant space to breathe, and you'll likely avoid powdery mildew.

Treat mildew with neem oil or copper fungicide, or use a mix of 1 tbsp baking soda, 1/2 tsp non-detergent soap, and a gallon of water, and spray this on. Try not to let the spray drip into the soil, and give your plant a good watering a few days later to flush out any residue.

Rust

Rust, again, looks just like its name – brown, rusty-looking rings or spots. It's more common in garden plants than on houseplants; if you do get it, treat it with copper spray or with sulfur powder. Sometimes, it's caused by letting the leaves stay wet for too long after watering; that's why watering the soil rather than the leaves, and being careful not to get succulent plants wet, is so important.

Sooty mold

Sooty mold looks nasty; it's black and powdery, often as if the edge of the leaf has been dipped in soot. In fact, if you have sooty mold, you have two problems, not one, because this mold is caused by pests such as thrips and scale insects. These bugs secrete 'honeydew,' a sticky substance on which the sooty fungus forms. So you need to eliminate the pests as well as the fungus, or the mold will just come back.

To treat the mold, remove the worst blighted leaves, and then wash your plants with household detergent in water; leave them for a quarter of an hour and then rinse off the detergent.

Leaf spots

Leaf spots could be related to a watering problem but can also show the plant is diseased. Leaf spots may occur because humidity or temperatures are too high, or because of poor air circulation.

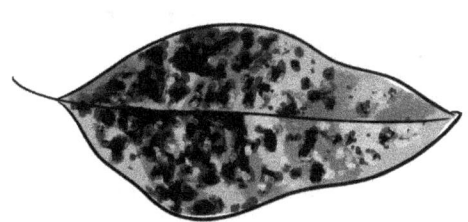

SOOTY MOLD

RUST

VIRUSES

You may also see mottled and streaky leaves. These generally mean your plant has a virus. Mottled discoloration, as if the leaves have been spattered with a different color paint, is often the sign of a mosaic virus, for which there's no cure. It's not that common in indoor plants, but it has been known to affect peace lilies, monstera and philodendrons. Viruses are highly contagious and unfortunately it's nearly impossible to save a plant once it has the virus.

You may, for once, have to sacrifice one of your plant babies. If you do, wrap the entire plant up together with all its soil and dispose of it securely (if you can have a bonfire in your garden, burn it); then wash your hands and any tools you used thoroughly, and put the pot in a diluted bleach solution.

A good way to prevent viruses arriving is to quarantine new plants for a few weeks, if you have the space. Spraying your plants from time to time with neem oil can also help protect your plants against diseases.

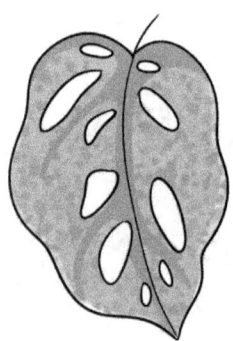

MOSAIC VIRUS

OTHER THINGS TO CONSIDER

Sometimes, a change in the color of leaves doesn't indicate a disease as such, but a nutrient deficiency. For instance, yellow or brown leaves can indicate the plant isn't getting enough nitrogen; yellow leaves turning to red or purple, or falling, might show the plant needs more potassium. Given a boost, your plant should recover, but this might be a sign that in the long term it needs a different fertilizer, repotting, or just more frequent feeding.

Basic hygiene can really help maintain disease-free houseplants. Wash your hands when you stop working on one plant, or pot, and start working on another; sterilize tools between plants with dilute bleach; remove dead leaves, flowers and branches; and keep your plants clean by spraying, dusting or brushing.

 ## PESTS

Houseplants are prone to a number of different types of pest. Many of them cause damage by biting into the plant and sucking out plant sap from the leaves. Scales, for instance, attach themselves permanently to the leaf once they are adult, and suck the sap; this eventually deforms the leaf, since the plant's energy is no longer getting to all parts of it. Spider mites bite into the leaf, which causes that part of the leaf to die and go brown.

Fungus gnats are innocent though annoying, but their larvae can damage plant roots, and often, they're connected with root rot; so if you see little black flies, stick a finger in the pot, and if the soil is squishy, examine the plant's roots.

A further way that pests can damage plants is through leaving sticky residues which can then be colonized by fungi like sooty mold. Aphids and mealybugs, for instance, emit honeydew (excreta), and that lets the fungus get established.

HOW TO IDENTIFY PESTS

Let's look at how you can identify these pests. One thing a lot of houseplant owners miss when they're looking for pests is the underside of leaves, so ensure you do turn the leaves over when you're checking your plants. You might actually see the bugs, or you might see other phenomena.

Symptom	Pest it could be	How to treat
'Cotton wool' on the leaf	Spider mite cobweb, mealybugs	Spider mites: They particularly like dracaenas, figs, and scheffleras; you can use a bit of dish soap and let it sit on the plant for a while, or use rubbing alcohol. Whichever you use, rinse it off in a couple of hours using tepid *water* and make sure the leaves dry out. Believe it or not, giving your plant a shower once a week can work! But (as always) make sure the leaves dry out afterwards, and use tepid water, not cold and certainly not boiling hot. Mealybugs: Mealybugs and scales are two kinds of sap-suckers. They are two different species but have similar habits, and the first sign of them may be sticky or waxy deposits on the plant. Mealybugs lay their eggs in white strands which can look a bit like cobweb, and particularly like poinsettias,

Symptom	Pest it could be	How to treat
		coleus, jade plant and hoya, orchids, succulents, and cacti. Scales, when adult, attach themselves to the plant and look like tiny brown scabs, often along the veins of a leaf; they prefer citrus and figs. Both mealybugs and scales can be eradicated with neem oil, insecticidal soap, or rubbing alcohol.
Tiny brown lumps along leaf veins and edges	Scale insects	Remove scale with a soft toothbrush or cotton swab dipped in soapy water or 70% isopropyl alcohol
Distorted leaves	Many different pests – the main one being thrips	Thrips: Use a blue or yellow sticky card and you'll soon see little, tiny thrips stuck to it. Under a loupe or microscope they look a bit like a lobster. Once you've found the thrips, prune off any affected leaves, and then use a mild treatment, such as insecticidal soap or neem oil spray. For really bad thrips infestations you could use a pyrethrin insecticide, unless you have cats. Pyrethrin is highly toxic to cats, though it's safe for dogs (that's one good reason you should never use dog flea treatments for a kitty, by the way)
Seeing pests on the underside of leaves or flying around above the soil	Aphids, fungus knats	Fungus knats: Yellow sticky traps, spot-wash the plant with isopropyl alcohol (rubbing alcohol) Aphids: See below

Symptom	Pest it could be	How to treat
Brownish dots (hold a piece of card underneath and knock the leaf gently, you may see little brownish dots fall off and start moving)	Spider mites	Use a bit of dish soap and let it sit on the plant for a while, or use rubbing alcohol. Whichever you use, rinse it off in a couple of hours and make sure the leaves dry out. Use tepid water, not cold and certainly not boiling hot
Sticky residue	Aphids	Easily detached from the leaf; just knock them into a saucer of soapy water, or even take the plant outside and give it a good spray with hose (though make sure it dries out properly). You can also spray with neem oil, or with soap and water spray.
Yellowing/ white leaves	Whiteflies	Whiteflies drink the plant's sap and as a result, the leaves will turn yellow and sometimes even white. Neem oil or insecticidal soap will deter these critters, but you may need to treat the plants weekly for a while.
Neem oil, insecticidal soap, and rubbing alcohol are great for all pests		

SPIDER MITE DAMAGE

Thrips are tiny, tiny things. You practically can't see them without a loupe, and they are the most dangerous of all these pests for your plants' health. Distorted leaves are often the first sign of thrips, which chew on your plant to make it bleed sap, and then suck up the sap. Streaking, browning and yellowing of leaves may also indicate a thrip problem.

OTHERS

Centipedes and millipedes are not particularly likely house guests unless you've left your plants outdoors for a while, and you're unlikely to find more than a couple. They live in wet soil. In fact, they do no harm to your plants; they're just creepy. If you find a couple, just pick them up and put them outside. If you are unlucky enough to keep finding more, then it's time to repot the plant and throw out the soil. Dunk the entire root ball in warm water and liquid soap for half an hour, then rinse well before repotting.

Snails and slugs, again, will probably only arrive if you left the plants outside for a while. Pick off any you see, take the plant outside and wash it carefully, and then scatter diatomaceous earth (DE) on the soil, as well as mixing it with water and spraying the plant. DE has really sharp edges and snails don't find it at all comfortable.

NATURAL TREATMENTS

Even if you're happy using chemical pesticides outdoors, using them in the home might make you think twice. They could affect your health or the health of your pets or children. So you might prefer to stick with treatments that either use common household resources or that are organic.

With any treatment, it's best to try it out on a few leaves first and wait a day or two before applying it all over, just in case the plant has a bad reaction.

NATURAL TREATMENT FOR PESTS

Neem oil

Neem oil is a natural insecticide that helps to stop the bugs from reproducing and spreading, as well as breaking down the outside layer of the insects. This is used by many houseplant-lovers as a long-term pest prevention and control method and is one of the best ways to help prevent bug infestations getting out of hand. Mix with water in a spray bottle and spray on the infected areas.

Dish-washing liquid

Dish-washing liquid or castile soap are very useful for getting rid of pests. It basically suffocates spider-mites, aphids, and mealybugs. You'll want to make sure your dish-washing liquid doesn't contain bleach, which is not good for your plants, and then dilute it heavily, with just one teaspoon of soap to a quart (or liter) of water. Spray the plant with it and you'll be getting rid of those pests.

Ground cinnamon

Ground cinnamon can be a houseplant parent's best friend. If you sprinkle it on the soil after watering, it soaks up any excess moisture and helps prevent over-watering. It also helps to prevent fungus gnats. It's surprisingly effective.

Canola oil

Half a cup of canola oil or another vegetable oil, mixed up with two tablespoons of dish-washing liquid, can be used to deter a number of bugs. Shake the mixture vigorously, as if you were making salad dressing, til it is well mixed and creamy, and then add a little water. Put it in a spray bottle and spray it on to the plant. The oil will block insects' spiracles (breathing holes) and they will suffocate.

Diatomaceous earth

Diatomaceous earth is made out of crushed fossil deposits, and as well as deterring snails and slugs, it can deter or kill all kinds of soft-bodied pests including ants, thrips, and mealybugs. Sprinkle it over the leaves and the soil. It can irritate if you breathe it in, so it's best to wear a mask while applying it; but once applied, it's entirely safe.

Chilli and garlic spray

Chilli and garlic spray is easy to make: blitz garlic and chilli peppers with water and allow the mixture to infuse overnight, then put it through a coffee filter, and spray the strained liquid over your plants. Remember not to rub your eyes when you're making or using this spray. You can also make a fungicidal spray from tomato leaves: chop them, pour boiling water over the top, leave for twenty-four hours and strain through a coffee filter, then spray your plants. Tomatoes contain the chemical tomatine, which is fungicidal and will also deter aphids.

Essential oil

Finally, if you're into essential oils, you can use a few drops of essential oil mixed with water to spray your plants. Thyme, peppermint, and lavender will all deter pests; so will tea tree oil, but this needs to be used in small quantities or it can be a bit too much for the plants.

ESCALATION!

Even those of us who are wedded to our home-made, non-chemical means of dealing with pests may decide to escalate to chemical controls if pests or diseases get out of hand, rather than lose our plants. There are a number of organic options available. Remember, though, that 'organic' doesn't mean 'non-toxic,' and it doesn't necessarily mean that undesirable side effects are absent (such as harmfulness to bees and other beneficial insects). Check the label; 'caution' is relatively safe, while 'danger' indicates a substance that could actually be deadly.

I would stick to 'caution'-level treatments. You should also check that whatever treatments you use are safe for indoor use. Again, you'll find that information on the label (if the weather is good, though, and you have a yard, why not take your houseplants outside to treat them, and bring them back in once it's been applied? That keeps any spray out of the air indoors). With sprays, it's a good idea to wear gloves, and also a mask so that you don't inhale any of the droplets.

Insecticidal granules and spikes are available, which you use scattered into the soil or pushed into the pot. The insecticidal compound enters the plant's roots, making the plant unappetizing to insects. This is reasonably safe to use, except on plants that you're going to eat, such as herbs.

Liquid copper fungicide, and sulfur fungicide, are both organic and safe methods of getting rid of rot and mildews. Make sure you use them in the correct concentration, as too much could burn leaves, and damage the plant.

PREVENTION

Dusting your plants really helps to keep them free from pests; it also means you're likely to notice pests quickly, before they become a big problem. Catching infestations early is key to keeping your plants healthy.

Other good plant hygiene includes tidying up fallen leaves; don't let them lie on the soil, where they could start rotting and encourage fungus. Keep your plants healthy and well fed and watered; many pests look for plants that are already weakened.

Spraying your plants with neem oil can help deter all kinds of critters. However, just pointing a spray bottle at the plant is not enough. You need to make sure to spray the undersides of the leaves, as this is where most of the bugs hang out.

 ## NUTRIENT DEFICIENCY

While yellowing leaves might be a sign of watering problems, or of disease, they might also indicate that the plant is not getting enough of one of its vital nutrients. Other signs could also indicate pests, or nutrient deficiency.

SIGNS OF NUTRIENT DEFICIENCY

- Yellow leaves, or yellow leaf edges.
- Brown leaf edges.
- Scorched leaves.
- Leaves that are turning purple or red.
- Yellowing between the leaf veins.
- Yellow or brown spots on the leaves.
- Twisted or deformed leaves.
- Small or stunted leaves.
- Holes in the leaves.

Since these symptoms might be due to watering issues, too much or too little light, disease, pests, *or* nutrient deficiency, you need to do some detective work. The first thing you should always do is check the moisture in the soil for watering problems. Then check the plant for pests, looking at the undersides of the leaves and using a sticky trap or shaking the plant over a card to see if thrips or spider mites fall out. If neither of these is the issue and you can't identify a fungal infection, then the next thing to do is to check the pH of the soil.

TESTING THE SOIL'S PH

pH is a measure of how acidic or alkaline the soil is. All plants have preferences, and if the soil isn't right for a plant that can affect its ability to access nutrients. You can either use testing strips or a hand-held probe to find out the soil's pH.

If you're using testing strips, you'll need to take some soil out of the pot, and mix it with twice as much distilled water as you have soil. Let it settle, and then test the liquid by dipping one of the strips into it. The strip will change color to show the pH, and you can compare it with the chart that comes with the strips. If you're using a probe, make sure the soil is moist first, then just stick the probe in the soil and the digital reading will show up in about a minute. That's not going to give you the most accurate reading that you could get – you'd need to go to a lab for that – but it should be close enough to be useful.

(If you're in any doubt about the meter, try putting it in water with vinegar, or in water with baking soda; that will show if it's adequately detecting acid from the vinegar, and alkali from the baking soda).

If the pH is wrong for the plant, it can be adjusted with lime or wood ash (to raise the pH and make it more alkaline), or with sulfur or aluminum sulfate (to lower the pH and make it more acidic). Work these materials into the soil; you only need a little.

If the pH is right, then you need to look for individual nutrient deficiencies. It's worth looking at your records and double checking the amount and type of fertilizer you have used on the plant. Check the concentration (did you give double strength fertilizer? Or not enough?) as well as the type of fertilizer.

SPECIFIC NUTRIENT DEFICIENCIES

Symptom	Deficiency it could be	How to fix
Yellowing leaves, paler leaves at the top of the plant, weak growth	Nitrogen	Use a nitrogen-specific additive rather than just increasing the regular fertilizer feed, or switch the plant to a nitrogen-heavy fertilizer. You could also mulch with organic matter such as compost
Older leaves going darker, purple or bronze fringes to the leaves, brown spots	Phosphorous	Mix some bone meal or phosphate rock into the soil. You might also consider a super-phosphate additive
Browning, burnt-looking leaf tips, purple spots, slow growth	Potassium	Add seaweed, kelp, or sulfate of potash, as well as perhaps fertilizing the plant in future with tomato feed (which has high levels of potassium)

Symptom	Deficiency it could be	How to fix
New growth is twisted, distorted, and leaf tips burnt	Calcium	Apply lime, bone meal, or gypsum to the soil. However, you need to be careful not to alter the soil pH too much in doing so. You could also use a calcium additive in water
Older leaves become very pale between the veins, like an 'arrowhead'	Magnesium	Spray on some Epsom salts mixed up in water. The plant will absorb the salts (basically magnesium sulfate) through the leaves quite quickly
Newer leaves look yellow (rather than the older leaves that show nitrogen deficiency)	Sulfur	Epsom salt spray

NITROGEN DEFICIENCY

CALCIUM DEFICIENCY

Nitrogen is responsible for leaf growth and the formation of chlorophyll, the green pigment in plants, which is why it causes leaf yellowing and weak growth.

Calcium is basic to cell formation. Magnesium is crucial for the process of photosynthesis, which is why, as with nitrogen deficiency, a plant that doesn't get enough magnesium will have pale, yellowing leaves.

Epsom salts spray will also help a sulfur deficiency. Since plants often have a deficiency of sulfur and nitrogen at the same time, it's worth giving Epsom salts when you're treating nitrogen deficiency, too.

Plants also need micro-nutrients such as zinc, boron, copper, iron, manganese, and molybdenum. Very quickly let's just run through the symptoms and treatment for each of these.

Symptom	Deficiency it could be	How to fix
Yellowing between veins of new leaves	Zinc	Add zinc chelates or zinc sulfate
Stunting and distortion of the growing tip that can lead to tip death, brittle foliage, and yellowing of lower leaf tips.	Boron	Add borax
Dark, stunted, drooping leaves	Copper	Add copper sulfate
The leaf goes yellow but the veins stay green	Iron	Add seaweed
Similar to a zinc deficiency	Manganese	Add sulfur
Older leaves have yellow spots	Molybdenum	Add chalk or limestone

NUTRIENT BOOSTS AND BALANCED FEEDING

The nutrient additions I just described are point solutions but, of course, over the long term, your plant needs a balance of nutrients. You don't want to go from just addressing one deficiency to addressing the next one; you want to ensure your plant is always getting the right nutrients. A big nutrient boost is great for a houseplant!

Outdoors, you'd add mulch and compost to replenish nutrients in the soil. For houseplants, repotting and feeding have to do the job. But there are some homemade nutrient mixes you can apply that will make a big difference.

If you have a wormery, you can use the liquid that comes out of the bottom ('vermicompost tea') diluted with ten parts water.

Simply water your plants with this every so often. If you don't have a wormery, you could pick up worm-casts (the little mounds of soil that earthworms excrete above ground) from the lawn; ask your local park warden if you can take theirs if you don' have a garden. Steep the worm casts in water overnight and then water the plants with the liquid.

You could also add a little compost on top of the soil and gently mix it with the top half inch of soil in the pot.

SUMMARY

The Appendix contains a table which is a roundup of the various symptoms of diseases, pests and deficiencies, together with the treatment for each one. This is a ready reference whenever one of your plants is looking poorly.

That was a rather depressing chapter. Still, apart from mosaic virus, almost all these problems can be successfully resolved if you catch them soon enough, which is why you want to check on your plants as often as you can. Don't forget to check the roots from time to time; if a plant's roots start to rot, you can rescue the plant by trimming the roots as long as you find out early enough. If the whole root ball has been attacked, it's almost impossible to save the plant (remember, too, that preventing root rot is all about not overwatering, so if you got things wrong in the past, you need to change your watering habits in future).

The next chapter, on the other hand, is going to be much more upbeat. It's all about how to increase your plant family by having lots of little plant babies – ways to create more plants from the ones you already have.

CHAPTER 8
PROPAGATION AND POTTING

I was horrified when my prize snake plant got root rot. I'd had it for years, and it had grown impressively tall – and though I managed to save it, I'd had to sacrifice over a third of the plant. It looked like a traumatized survivor, and I certainly was traumatized; I'd come so close to losing it.

Fast forward a few years and not only has that plant recovered, I'm surrounded by its children and grandchildren too. Worried that I might not be able to save my plant, I took cuttings from some of the unaffected leaves, snipped them up, and planted them in moist soil. They grew! Later, I grew a second generation, and I've even been able to swap some of my babies with other growers for different species of snake plant.

But that's still a tiny achievement compared with one woman in Mississippi who grew *sixty* new fiddle leaf figs from one parent plant.

Propagating is not that hard to do, and it's particularly easy to get started because the easiest to grow plants are also the easiest plants to propagate. You'll be able to increase your plant collection, and you'll learn even more about how to provide ideal conditions for your plants as you grow new ones. It can save you money on new plants, or let you produce presents for friends and family.

Propagation is basically plant breeding or reproduction. Most of us know about how to grow plants from seeds; maybe you grew mustard and cress on the windowsill as a kid, or maybe you're fed up with pulling baby sycamore trees out of your lawn, where their propeller-shaped seed cases brought them. But there are other ways to propagate, such as from leaf or stem cuttings, root cuttings, or by dividing plants. For house plants, these approaches are often more successful than growing from seed.

It's a bit of challenge. Just like human babies, plant babies need more attention than adults. A mistake that a fully grown plant would survive could kill a young cutting. And even if you do well, you'll probably never have a 100% success rate; there will always be a few plants that don't make it. Some plants are better propagators than others: spider plant, pothos and snake plant will give you a great rate of success.

PROPAGATING

There are a few basic things that you need to get right when you're propagating.

PROPAGATING MUST-DOs

1. Always use fresh potting compound and use a seed potting compound rather than the mix you use for your mature plants.
2. Use a rooting hormone to increase your success rate, or if you want to be 100% natural, use aloe vera gel, which has the same effect of promoting rooting.
3. Use a heated propagating mat to get the soil temperature right and ensure your babies get off to a good start.
4. Above all, keep everything squeaky clean, from your hands and tools to your pots and compost.

PROPAGATING USING A HEAT MAT

You can also propagate in water. I find that more exciting, as I can see the roots start to appear and follow the plant's growth day by day, but it does mean I have to transfer the plants to soil once their root system has developed. If you propagate in soil, you won't have to transfer til the plant is ready for its own pot.

Another advantage of propagating in water is that it can actually look quite attractive – a wall-mounted propagation rack can make a fascinating decorative feature.

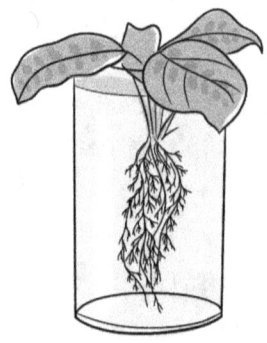

PROPAGATING IN WATER

If you want to experiment, try both soil and water propagation for cuttings from the same plant, and compare your success with each method - not just how many plants you end up with, but how fast and how large they grow.

You can propagate using different parts of the plant. Some plants can only be propagated one way, while others have a number of different ways that you can propagate them. Again, for plants that have a number of different ways to propagate, why not experiment and see which works best for you?

OFFSETS

Some plants form tiny side shoots around the base. These are called offsets, and each of them has the ability to become a new plant. Plants which propagate through offsets include:

- Echeveria
- Haworthia
- Urn plant
- Aloe

Remove each offset carefully, making sure that it has some roots attached. The offsets should have been growing for a few months, so they're big enough to survive on their own. Cut the offsets off cleanly with a sharp knife and let them dry out a little to form a callus over the wound before you put them in compost (most succulents which produce offsets don't prosper with water propagation).

LEAF CUTTINGS

Lots of plants can be propagated through leaf cuttings. For instance, you can take a leaf from Christmas cactus, echeveria, jade plant, ZZ plant, snake plant, or begonias. In the case of the snake plant, you can even cut one big leaf into smaller parts and plant them separately (don't separate the leaves of plants like Christmas cactus, which grow in sections; remove the whole section).

Let the raw edge dry off by leaving it a day or so, and then pot it in compost, with the raw edge in the soil. Keep most of the leaf above the ground.

Some plants can be treated slightly differently. African violet leaves can be placed with the stems in a pot of water till they form leaves. With begonias, cut through some of the leaf veins, and pin the leaf down on to your potting compost with toothpicks; roots will then start to grow from the cuts where they touch the compost. Once plantlets have formed, you can repot them.

STEM CUTTINGS

Stem cuttings are a good way to propagate plants that grow on stems or like trees, such as monstera, palms, yucca, and vines like pothos. Geroniums also do well with stem cuttings.

Stem cuttings are a good way to use prunings when you have to prune down a 'leggy' cane or tree but they are also a good way to propagate a plant that is no longer growing well at the top ("going bald" as one of my friends says). Cut the cane you've pruned into pieces about as long as your middle finger and push them into the compost. Make sure the cane is still the same way up as it was on the plant.

PROPAGATING USING STEM CUTTINGS

Stem cuttings from pothos, monstera, philodendrons and ZZ plants can do well in water.

ROOT, RHIZOME AND TUBER PROPAGATION

Some plants will propagate from a root cutting, or from a rhizome or tuber. Technically these are different parts of a plant, but basically let's group them together because they are all underground.

Root cuttings can be taken by cutting off one branch of the main root and chopping it into two-inch sections. Each section can then be planted in compost; make sure it points the right way up (i.e. the same way it was in the pot).

Rhizome division works well with plants like ZZ plant, which grow from rhizomes (horizontal underground stems). Cleanly cut the rhizome, making sure that each section you cut has some root and some leaf emerging from it. An interesting rhizome plant you might want to try growing is ginger; if you see a sprout emerging from the ginger root in your kitchen, have a go. It's an attractive plant and should yield you plenty more ginger for cooking with or making into candied ginger.

You may already have an idea of how tuber division works if you've ever grown potatoes. Tubers grow a number of 'eyes' which eventually become sprouts. You can cut the tuber into several pieces as long as you ensure that each section has an 'eye.' This works well for tuberous begonia and caladium plants.

Some plants, like alocasia, have corms, which look like little balls hanging from the roots. If you delve through the roots of a mature plant, you'll probably find a number of these corms, which you can plant, and which will eventually grow into new plants identical to the parent.

ZZ PLANT TUBERS

PLANTLETS

Some plants create plantlets at the end of long flowering stems, or 'runners.' These are basically tiny adult plants; they grow their roots while they're hanging at the end of the stem, so they're ready to go straight into compost at that point (don't confuse them with offsets – offsets grow around the base of the parent plant, while plantlets are separated from the parent by the 'runner').

Moth orchids create plantlets on some of their flower spikes and can be propagated, though it can take several years for the new plants to flower. The plantlet-propagating plant everyone knows, though, is the spider plant, and that's definitely the easiest one to start with. Simply cut the plantlet off the stem cleanly, then plant it in a standard compost mix, covering the roots up.

LAYERING

Layering is a way of using the vine or runner of a plant to produce new plantlets. Using layering, you don't cut into the plant at all; instead, you simply pin down part of the vine stem into a compost-filled pot with a hairpin. The stem needs to be below the compost at that point to make it root.

Layering is low-risk, as the mother plant will still be feeding the plantlet till it gets large enough to be self-sufficient. At that point you can cut it loose and repot it, if necessary. Ivy, pothos, and spider plants can all be layered (though I wouldn't go to the extra trouble for spider plants).

For plants with tough stems, cut upwards into the stem, just below a leaf node. Only cut a little less than halfway, then keep the cut open by inserting a toothpick. Brush a little hormone rooting powder into the cut. Then get some sphagnum moss or peat compost, wet it, and pack it round the cut inside a plastic bag. Tie the bag to the stem with plastic ties. Ensure it is kept moist, and eventually you'll see roots forming. Once the roots are clearly developed, you can cut the new plant off. The mother plant will look rather sad for a while, but will grow back in time.

DIVISION

Plants like ferns, cast iron plant, peace lilies, elephant's ear and snake plants grow in clumps with a number of stems. These plants can be propagated by division. Remove the plant from the pot, and gently tease the clump apart from the roots, dividing it into individual plants. With a sharp knife, divide off those plants that have their own sets of roots, and then plant them in their own pots.

This can be a fairly messy process, so it's best to do it outside, or lay down plastic sheet or paper before you get started so that you can pull all the mess together once you're finished.

GROWING MEDIUM

With all styles of propagation, if you're using soil rather than water, you should choose a 'rooting' or 'seed planting' compost, and remember to keep it moist (you're going to need to do this for a couple of months, so don't try to take cuttings just before your vacation). Or you can mix your own growing medium, using any of the following:

GROWING MEDIUMS

- Soil, perhaps mixed with peat moss or perlite to help keep it moist.
- LECA, clay balls that absorb moisture and release it gradually. LECA is sterile, and cleaner to use than soil.
- Perlite can be used on its own when you are taking root cuttings, or with a little sphagnum moss mixed in. It's a great moisture retainer, and provides more aeration than vermiculite (another possible medium).
- Coconut coir is a great growing medium, but needs watering at least once a day since it doesn't retain moisture particularly well. Coco coir mixed with perlite might be a better mix unless you are very attentive to your babies. It's best used with cuttings that want to remain wet.

- Sphagnum moss is particularly good for woody stem cuttings. It's one of the best water-retention media, and lets air as well as water get to the roots. Peat moss is also a good medium but I prefer not to use it owing to its environmental sensitivity (many peat bogs, which are a rare ecosystem, are being destroyed by over-extraction).
- Sand works for many root cuttings, such as succulents. It may be best to add a little potting mix, helping it to retain more water. Because it doesn't clump up, it allows the roots space to grow. It's perfect for cuttings that need not to be too wet, such as cacti and succulents.

HOW TO CHOOSE YOUR PROPAGATION METHOD

As you may have noticed, some plants are much easier to propagate by a certain method, such as snake plants by leaf propagation or division. Effectively, you're taking advantage of the way the plant would naturally propagate in the wild and accelerating the process. So if you see a plant producing plantlets or offsets, you pretty much know that this would be a good way to propagate.

But many plants will let you propagate them in a number of different ways. For instance, succulents will propagate through leaf cuttings or root cuttings. They will also propagate in water, though if you choose water as a growing medium, you need to put the plants into soil once the roots are half an inch long.

Fiddle-leaf figs will propagate through leaf cuttings and stem cuttings. However, the failure rate for leaf cuttings is much higher (I couldn't find out how many failures the lady with sixty fiddle-leaf babies had experienced but I bet it was a big number).

If you're propagating in water, remember that the water needs changing every few days – three or four days maximum – to avoid it becoming slimy.

THE CHALLENGES OF PROPAGATION

Challenge	How to overcome
Most cuttings need to be kept in high humidity conditions; 80-85% or even 100% (like your bathroom when you're taking a hot shower)	Putting a plastic bag over the pot to make a mini-greenhouse is one way of ensuring humidity is high; you could also consider buying a propagation tray with a fitted lid which will keep the water vapor in
Keeping everything scrupulously clean – high temperatures and humidity make ideal conditions for diseases to get established	Always clean your tools and containers before using them, and use fresh growing medium
Some plants are quite hard to propagate. Variegated plants will sometimes revert to solid green in plants taken from cuttings. Variegation is a mutation that can be more or less stable	You'll only find out the stability factor of any given variety by experience

Challenge	How to overcome
Some succulents are also unexpectedly challenging. Haworthia, for instance, has a high failure rate, which is a pity, as it's a real stunner of a plant	Experience!

GROWING PLANTS FROM SEED

Some houseplants will grow from seed. For instance, most herbs will grow from seed. You can even buy pots already sown with seed which just need you to open the package, put the pots on your windowsill, and water them. Cat grass is another plant that grows well from seed. Among other houseplants, you could try African violet, English ivy, coleus, living stones, and peace lilies.

There are a couple of disadvantages to growing from seed. One is that houseplant seeds generally don't store well. Another is that germination times (the time it takes for the seed to develop root and stem beginnings) can be quite long, so you could spend three months waiting to see any development. Cuttings have usually started developing nicely within a couple of weeks.

However, seeds are much easier to share than cuttings. For instance, you could put seeds in the post, or hand an envelope to a friend.

HOW TO GROW FROM SEED

What you'll need:

- A small container with drainage hole or a seed tray/paper pots
- Seeds
- Labels

Method:

1. To plant seeds, you'll first want to fill a container with growing medium. Make sure the container has at least one drainage hole. You can use a seed tray, planting pots, make recycled newspaper pots, or use old yogurt pots, egg cartons, or eggshells (an advantage to paper pots is that repotting is easy – you don't have to take the plant out of the pot, just bury the pot in the new compost and it will rot away in time).

2. Then, before you take the seeds out of the packet, water

the growing medium thoroughly and let it drain.

3. Sow the seeds, and cover lightly with a little more medium. It's suggested you bury them three times their own depth, but many are so small that you might as well leave them uncovered (be careful to read the instructions; some seeds need darkness to germinate).

4. Keep the soil moist and warm, and... wait!

5. Don't forget to label your pots. With cuttings, you might be okay as you can see what plant you've got in front of you, but if you don't label seed trays, you won't know what on earth the plant is that's emerging from the soil!

6. Once the seeds have sprouted, you need to give them light. Without fairly bright light, they will grow leggy and pale, and may die off early. Once the seedlings have developed a couple of pairs of leaves, they're ready to be transplanted. Be careful to hold them gently by their leaves and try not to disturb the root ball.

GROWING FROM SEED

 ## THE ART OF REPOTTING — ADVANCED!

Sometimes a plant will outgrow its pot. In the wild, a plant can freely extend its roots wherever it wants; a houseplant doesn't have this option. The pot can become a real threat to its growth and even to its health, since the roots will in the end fill the pot, making proper drainage impossible.

That's why as a rule of thumb, gardeners say you should repot plants every six months to a year, when they're young and growing fast, and other plants every few years. You should also try to keep a good ratio between the pot and the plant; for upright growth plants, the plant should be about twice as high as its pot.

But while that's good practice, you ought to be able to recognize when plants are crying out for your help. Signs that a plant desperately needs a larger pot include:

- A marked slow-down in its growth rate.
- Suddenly yellowing leaves.
- Roots finding their way out of the pot, over the side or through the drainage hole.
- The plant not getting enough water even though its watering schedule hasn't changed.
- Sudden leaf drop.
- Salt deposits visible on top of the soil.
- Water resting on the soil when you water, and not penetrating underneath.
- The plant falling over because it's top-heavy.

If any of these things are happening, ease your plant gently out of the pot to sneak a peek at the roots. If the roots are going round and round in circles, your plant is going crazy from confinement – please give it more room in a bigger pot!

Don't repot a plant you have only just bought or been gifted. It's already adjusting to its new growing conditions, so leave it a few weeks to get adjusted before you think about giving it a new pot.

Usually, plants are repotted into a bigger pot. But if, say, you've just got your monstera the right size to fit behind the sofa and not hit the ceiling, you could keep your plant the same size by pruning the roots, then repotting it in the same pot.

Make sure when you're repotting that the soil is the right kind for the plant. Orchids need a lot of tree bark mixed in; cacti and succulents need soil that drains freely, with plenty of perlite, vermiculite, pumice, or gravel. Don't use garden soil, because if you do, you can bring in blights and diseases, bugs, slugs, and snails, but it's also likely to become compacted very easily, making it easy to over-water your plants.

There's no need to add fertilizer when you repot. The potting mix is full of nutrients, anyway, and the plant needs to recover gently without any extra stimulation. Just remember to moisten the potting mix a little before you start, so that the plant can get at oxygen and nutrients.

If your plant has plantlets or offsets in addition to having outgrown its pot, this might be a good time to propagate them. In that case, ensure you have smaller containers for the babies, and enough potting mix to fill them.

Water leafy plants the night before repotting and give them another dose in the morning. Once they're out of the pot, prune the tips of the roots (this is something my granddad used to do for apple trees!) as this will stimulate growth.

Post-repotting care and acclimatization are important. Repotting can be traumatic for the plant, so you need a 'convalescent dorm' for repotted plants. Help your houseplant recover from the disturbance by giving it a good watering and then dialing down the light a bit, which is equivalent to saying "Have a nice sleep, now."

Repotting cuttings is just the same as repotting bigger plants, just remember these are still babies. You won't want to do any pruning on the cuttings, though, and you'll want to make really sure the potting mix is nice and moist.

MAKE YOUR OWN GROWTH MEDIUM FOR REPOTTING

Plenty of people buy their potting mix, but you might like to try something different. By selecting the right ingredients and mixing in different ratios, you can suit the mix to the plant that you're repotting. Tailor-made potting mix makes for happier plants.

Start with a basis of coconut coir fiber. It's a bit more expensive than peat moss, but it's far more sustainable, and the expense is worth it as coir will last much longer, too. Also, it has a neutral pH, whereas peat is acidic. You'll find most of these products in good garden centers, but you can even order them from Amazon nowadays!

Now think about what you want to add.

- Perlite. It's actually a volcanic rock, which is heated up (like popcorn!) to make little puffs. It's very lightweight, sterile, and vastly improves drainage.

- Vermiculite. Like perlite, it's made from mined materials puffed up by heat into super-light fragments. It increases the porosity of the mix and helps drainage, and also adds calcium and magnesium.

- Sand can improve drainage, but make sure you use coarse (sharp), not fine or builders' sand. This is a good addition for cacti.

- Fertilizers. So far, the growing medium doesn't contain much in the way of nutrients. You can add your own mix of cottonseed meal, bone-meal, and kelp or seaweed, or you can buy a complete organic fertilizer. These need adding in small amounts – a cup of fertilizer is good enough for 12 gallons of potting medium!

- Composted wood chips or wood chip mulch can help when you have shrubs and trees that have grown massive, as it's a way of filling big pots while keeping the weight down. Add some blood meal to boost nitrogen, as wood chips will use nitrogen when they break down.

- Compost is great stuff for potting mix, though not for seed starting.

RECIPE FOR DIFFERENT PLANTS

A general recipe that works well for most houseplants (other than orchids, cacti and succulents) is:

- 6 parts each of coir and compost.
- A couple of spoonfuls of fertilizer.
- 4 parts perlite.

For instance, if you're starting off with a spider plant or two, this would be quite suitable. ZZ plant and snake plant would also be quite happy with it.

For trees and shrubs, use:

- 6 parts each of coir.
- 6 parts compost.
- 6 parts perlite.
- 5 parts coarse sand.
- 5 parts composted bark.
- Add some fertilizer.

And for cacti, a good starting mix might be:

- 3 parts coir.
- 2 parts sand.
- 2 parts of vermiculite or perlite (or a mix of the two).

You might also try a simple mix of 4 parts coir to 3 parts perlite, with a small addition of coarse sand. Most succulents also prefer this type of mix.

Orchids need something quite different:

- 3 parts bark.
- 1 part perlite.
- 1 part chopped sphagnum moss, or 5 parts of bark to 1 of coco coir.
- You might also add a little fine charcoal. But orchids are such a specialty that you're probably better off buying your orchid potting compound ready-made.

Once you've started making your own potting mixes, and you're repotting and propagating your own plants, you've become a houseplant expert. I bet you have discovered that 'green thumb' you thought you didn't have!

That's why the last chapter is about taking things to the next level – specialized areas from orchids to hydroponics, creating terrariums, and nurturing the most exotic kinds of plants.

CHAPTER 9
AUTOMATION AND ARTIFICIAL LIGHTING

 AUTOMATING THE INDOOR GARDEN

There are a number of ways you can automate your houseplant care regime. Some of these methods are quite old tech, for instance, terracotta watering spikes which can hold a week's worth of water, and the glitzier-looking glass watering globes which work on the same basis. You can also use drip systems and wick systems for watering. With all these systems, it's important that you soak the soil well first and let it start to drain. You'll then set up the spike, or wick. Because the soil is moist, the spike/wick won't start to provide water to the soil until some has been absorbed or evaporated.

These systems are not suitable for plants like cacti, succulents, orchids, or other plants that like to dry out before being watered again. They do take some of the work out of watering those plants that like the soil to be continuously moist.

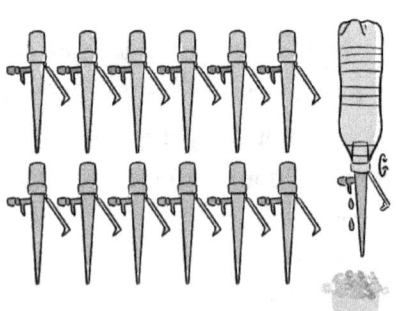

SPIKE WATERING SYSTEM

WICK SYSTEM

MAKE YOUR OWN WATER SYSTEMS

<u>Spike system</u>

1. Get a small plastic soda bottle. Poke or drill a couple of holes in the cap.
2. Fill the bottle with water and turn it upside down into the soil. You could also use a wine bottle – cover the end with saran wrap and poke a couple of holes in.
3. You can also buy ready-made spikes made of plastic, terracotta or even glass, which you can poke into the soil once full of water, and which will gradually drip water for your plants. Look for 'watering spikes' or 'watering globes' and you'll find there is a lot of choice.

<u>Wick system</u>

You can buy wick systems, but you can also create one yourself. The idea is that the wick gradually soaks up water from a container and through capillary action, transmits it to the plant pot. Because the wick uses capillary action, it can bring water up from a lower level.

A really easy way to make a wick system is to use a piece of string or a strip cut from an old t-shirt. Fill an old teacup or a yogurt pot, or whatever you have to hand, with water, and put this next to the plant pot. Put one end of the wick into the water pot, and the other end into the soil in the plant pot.

Or, if your plants are in the kitchen, you could use your kitchen sink as the container for the water. You can also use a capillary mat as the wick; the advantage of these mats is that you can feed a whole lot of plants at one time just by placing the pots on the mat. As the soil in the pots dries out, it will naturally suck up moisture from the mat. Most good garden centers sell capillary mats, sometimes as part of a kit including a water tank and plant stand; they're easy to find online, too.

For neatness, you can adjust the wick system by stacking one container inside another. For instance, I have sometimes used three pots – a waterproof outside pot which contains an inch or so of water in the bottom, a small pot upside down as a stand, and the plant pot set on that pot so that its bottom is out of the water. Then I just add a strip of fabric inside to bring the water to the plant pot, but it's all hidden by the big outside container, so it looks just like an ordinary planter.

A friend of mine has a less-aesthetic system which also works well. He cuts soda bottles in two. In the bottom half of the bottle he puts some water. He turns the neck of the bottle upside down, plugs the neck with a strip of cotton, and fills it with soil, then puts this into the other container (it's important to make sure the water doesn't reach the bottom of the bottle neck, but does touch the cotton wick). Then whatever plant he puts in the pot will get fed with water.

Wick systems are also great for when you're on vacation – if you have thirsty plants that need more regular watering, this is the perfect solution to keeping them hydrated while you're away.

If all of this is too much for you, you can buy 'self-watering pots,' which are essentially just wick systems that have already been set up for you. Some of them are really quite pretty, particularly the glass ones where you can see the plant roots and the water.

Others

If you don't have a sink with a draining board to use a capillary mat (or if you prefer to keep the draining board clear of plants), you can make a similar system using a tray of water with a block of Styrofoam to support the pots out of the water.

Or you could simply fill the bath tub with a few inches of water and put your plant pots in the water. However, this is only viable for plants which don't need dry soil, and as with the other systems you need to water the plants first. While these ways of minimizing watering seem like great news, you need to be very careful about what kind of plants you use them on, or you'll be getting root rot and seeing plants die. No wicking system will help you with succulents and cacti, because they don't like to have moist soil at all.

SELF WATERING POT

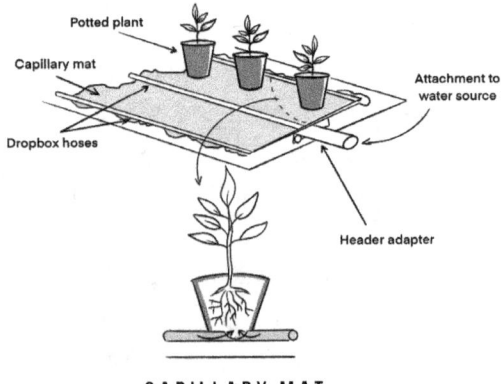

CAPILLARY MAT

OTHER IRRIGATION STRATEGIES

Irrigation systems are great for the garden, and potentially disastrous for houseplants. Just using a drip system to drip water in a pot is a sure-fire way to over-water, and potentially kill, your plants. Such systems work outside because the soil is deep and can absorb vast amounts of water – they don't work so well for a pot where the absorption capacity is finite.

For plants which need humidity in the air and also need moisture in the soil, making a mini greenhouse is a good solution. Simply fit a clear plastic bag over the plant and tie it gently closed. It's best to puff some air in before you tie it up, so that the bag doesn't touch the plant. When the water evaporates from the soil, the vapor will hit the bag, turn back into drops of water, and fall back to water the plant. It's a neat system but it has one shortcoming: if you put it in the sun, it will act like a magnifying glass or an oven! In a later chapter, I'll talk about terrariums, which are basically rather more sophisticated versions of the plant-in-a-bag mini greenhouse.

Another way to make watering last a little longer is to use watering crystals. These are polymer crystals that are mixed into the potting soil, and which soak up moisture in order to release it gradually. They basically increase the water holding capacity of the soil, meaning you can go longer between waterings.

If you want to go high tech, you could use smart home automated systems, which have a central reservoir and individual settings for each plant. They'll cost $50-100, against smaller systems that don't have the ability to change the settings for each plant, but that's worth the investment if you have less common or more expensive plants, or just a lot more plants. Or you could group plants with similar needs together and use a system without individual controls, because you'll only need to use one setting for all your plants. You can also run two or three feeds to your biggest plants and a feed each for the smaller ones, so that the bigger plants are getting two or three times more water.

From here, you *might* want to move on to a full hydroponic drip system, in which the pump feeds plants with both water and nutrients. You will need a dedicated drip emitter for each plant, which needs a timer system fitted to it (otherwise it will keep going until the plants are completely drowned). This requires a good deal of planning and installation time up front. Excess water is allowed to drain back into the system for re-use.

The difficulty with such a system is that since it provides nutrients, you can't mix plants which need different nutrients in the same system, such as plants that need nitrogen-rich fertilizer with ones that need nitrogen-poor fertilizer.

You'll need DIY skills to make your own hydroponic system, but all the components are easy to get: thin tubing, drip emitters, larger PVC tubing for the main lines, a water pump, a large water bucket, a garden timer, silicone sealant, and a hydroponic growing medium like coco coir, rather than soil, for your plants.

If you do automate, make sure you run a trial of the system before you run it for real. Finding out that it doesn't work properly while you're at home is fine; finding out it doesn't work when you come back from two weeks in Mexico is heart-rending.

If you're worried about watering when you're only away for a week or a long weekend, though, you don't need these systems, because a low-tech approach is a much simpler answer. If you water all the plants before going, put them in lower than usual light conditions and in a cooler place than they're used to, and put a bit of mulch on top of the soil to stop evaporation, they'll be okay. Because they've been put in lower light and cooler conditions, they won't consume as much water as usual. You can make mulch from coir fiber, coir, pebbles, marbles, tree bark, or even pistachio shells – just don't let it pile up against the stem of the plants.

Or you could have a plant buddy pop in. If you do, help them by grouping your plants according to their watering needs, and leaving specific instructions. If you want to get things perfect, you should actually measure how much water you give each plant, over a period of a month or so before you go away, but if your plant buddy knows which plants need which kind of watering treatment, you'll be fine.

ARTIFICIAL LIGHTING

Artificial lighting can be great where you don't get a lot of natural light in your home. It's definitely not as powerful as natural light but can definitely help with growth and flowering. Lacking light can be one of the most common ailments that negatively affects houseplants so artificial might be the key to helping them thrive as one of the easiest and least expensive ways of providing light.

The human eye is a poor judge of light intensity because it automatically adjusts to different levels of light. Calculating wattage per square foot of growing area is one of the easiest ways to estimate the light required. When using fluorescent tubes, you simply multiply the wattage desired by square foot of growing area. An example may be if you have a 4 square-foot area of low-light plants that need 10 watts of light, you would calculate 10 watts x 4 square feet or 40 watts.

Grow lights help plants to photosynthesize by mimicking the sun's full spectrum or by emitting wavelengths in the red or blue ranges. The light therefore provides food for them to grow and flower. Regular house bulbs may give us light in our homes but they are no good for plants, which need blue and red light to grow. Blue is important for growth and red for flower production but a bit of both is needed for healthy and balanced growth.

Artificial lighting is simple to install, and can be of varied complexity and cost, depending on your needs. You can get a light bulb that prioritizes red- and blue-spectrum light from about $10 upwards; these are simple to install and will fit in virtually any lamp. That's the least intrusive way of lighting as it lets you use your existing light fittings, and it's also efficient because it doesn't waste energy giving your plants a lot of 'white' light they can't use.

But there could be better options. Let's take a look at these below.

FULL SPECTRUM LED GROW LIGHT

ARTIFICIAL LIGHTING

1. **Incandescent lights**. This is a poor source of light for plants, they have a lot of red light but not much blue. And the bulbs are too hot to put close to the plant. The bulbs are inefficient users of energy and have a short life. In summary, you don't want incandescent lights.

2. **Fluorescent tubes.** This is a good light source for plants and is more than twice as efficient in energy use than incandescent lighting. Purchase tubes that are specifically intended for growing plants and focus on the red/blue spectrum; you can use these in combination with the white or daylight tubes you use for regular lighting, for instance in the kitchen. Most horticultural suppliers will have these available in all different shapes and sizes. They are long-lasting (most last about 20,000 hours) and economic to run. Unlike incandescent lights, they give off relatively little heat so you can put them close to the plants. If you position them correctly, they will be strong enough to help your plants grow and flower.

3. **High-intensity discharge (HID).** HID lamps using sodium or metal halide are often used in greenhouses and are four times more efficient than fluorescent lamps. However, they emit a lot of heat, and are expensive and bulky, needing extraction equipment to remove the hot air.

So they're not really suitable for home use.

4. **Light-emitting diodes (LEDS)** are long-lived and extremely efficient. As with fluorescent tubes, you can buy LEDs specifically designed for plant growing. LEDs can be expensive but prices have come way down as more people use them, and they are great for home use as they come with domestic-styled fittings. They benefit from low operating temperatures and are even longer lasting than fluorescents. Specialist light meters may also be needed to measure their light output which can make them more expensive to set up. They can also be placed close to the plant so you don't need to worry about burning the leaves.

5. **Spotlights** can also be used but are not the most effective since the majority are incandescent and therefore not energy efficient and give off a lot of heat, without a good balance of red and blue light. Some self-reflectorized spot lamps which emit more blue light are available but other options are generally better.

HOW TO USE ARTIFICIAL LIGHTS

Tubes that have a 4000k value tend to produce light that has a reddish tone, whereas those at 7500k produce bluish light. If you decide to use fluorescent tubes, a combination of both blue and red light will give your plants the best chance to flower and grow. Most residential, small-scale applications and full-spectrum LED lights are the best option due to them being energy efficient and offering the full spectrum range that plants need.

It is also important to have the lights on for a sufficient number of hours. If you are just supplementing natural light with artificial lighting, you would normally give them twelve to fourteen hours; you don't want to run them round the clock. If you are replacing natural light, you might want to give them sixteen to eighteen hours a day (depending on the plant's requirements). Plants will always need a daily rest cycle so never keep them under grow lights all day and night.

You might want to consider putting your grow lights on a timer so that you don't forget to turn them off. This is also good for when you're away from the house for long periods.

There are simple kits out there for beginners to start with and a simple home set up could be two 60cm fluorescent tubes suspended 60cm above the plants, with the lights on for between twelve to eighteen hours a day (depending on requirements).

If you are using grow lights for seedlings, you will want to use blue light for growth. Place fluorescent tubes 60cm above the plants. These are great for tomatoes seedlings for example, which are often started early in the season when natural light levels are low.

Lights for plants should be installed quite close to the plant (ideally 1 foot away from the tips because the intensity of light drops rapidly the further away the light is) to ensure they get enough light. It's useful if you can move the lights around so that the plant doesn't start growing in a single direction. The middle part of a fluorescent tube is also the strongest so place your plants as close to the middle as possible. It is best to have moveable fixings so that you can adjust the distance easily when needed.

For most plants, ensure you place the lights directly above the plant so that it grows upwards rather than sideways to 'reach' the light. For other species such as trailing varieties, it is not as important since they don't need to grow upwards.

Reflectors and reflective surfaces can maximize the amount of light a plant will receive and some bulbs have self-contained reflectors built in. Some reflectors are porcelain-coated and require little maintenance. Make sure you keep them clean and free of dust. Use white paint or aluminum foil beneath to help reflect light more effectively. Also make sure that plants are spaced far enough apart that they are not shading each other.

Given their low prices, energy efficiency and ease of use, fluorescent lights are the first choice for many houseplant growers. Cool-white tubes remain the most popular but warm-white are effective too. Those listed as white or daylight don't tend to have enough red rays for plants to grow.

Tubes that are developed specifically for growing plants have a higher red light output to balance the blue light. These can be used with cool-white tubes; use one plant-growing tube to every two cool-white tubes for the best effect. The cool-white tubes cost less than the plant-growing ones, and plant-growing tubes use less electricity than the less popular incandescent bulbs.

HANGING GROW LIGHT

HOW MUCH LIGHT DO PLANTS NEED?

Different plants often require different light intensities. The foliage color can be a good indicator to determine if they are receiving enough light.

House plants are generally categorized into three different categories; low, medium and high light intensities which indicates the minimum light requirement.

It is important to research the light requirements of each plant as they all have different light requirements. For example, moth orchids and African violets are easy to grow under lights and are tolerant of many different light conditions. When thriving, their leaves will be a mid-green color.

Plants that usually live in low-light habitats such as ferns and tropical plants can thrive long-term quite easily using simple artificial lighting. These can be placed in an aquarium tank that can be used as a terrarium with the fluorescent lights placed in the hood. This will help to retain high humidity which these plants love. Low-light plants should receive between 10 and 15 watts of fluorescent light per square foot of growing space. If you just use one fluorescent tube (such as a 2-foot 20-watt tube) it will provide just enough light for plants in the low light category.

Medium light intensity plants need at least 15 watts per square foot of growing area but if you want optimal growth and flowering, you should use more than this. A fixture containing two tubes is sufficient.

For plants with high light requirement, you will need to use a lot more intensity and at least 200 watts per square foot, even more if you want optimal growth. Fixtures containing three or four tubes are ideal here.

If you want to light a particular area, such as a table with a number of plants on it, you might consider a hanging grow light. Some of these can be tricky to install, with a number of different wires to be attached, and are probably not for renters; others can be hung from a stand, or from an S-hook on a shelf. While some hanging lights are intended for use in hothouses, others have minimalist designs that look great in the home. These lights used to be very expensive but now are available for as little as $30. Good ones will last for years.

For tall plants, you may want to place spotlights around their base directed on the lower leaves or use tubes up the side of the plant to provide side lighting.

You might also look at clip-on grow lamps, which are similar to clip-on desk lamps, just with more red- and blue-spectrum light. They're easy to set up, and since they're so easily portable, it's great to have a few of them so you can use them tactically anywhere a plant isn't getting quite enough light.

Complete indoor garden units are available which water and light your plants automatically. They're often intended for growing herbs indoors but they're not very flexible; you have a certain number of slots to fill, and that's it. Personally, I feel you'd be better off learning how to be a better plant parent, save the money and spend it later on getting more plants.

PROBLEMS YOU MAY ENCOUNTER

If you see that the leaves nearest to the lights start to go yellow-green, this could be an indication that the light intensity is too high for that particular plant. There are a number of things you can do here. You can reduce the number of tubes or position them further away from the plant. You can also reduce the number of hours the plants are exposed to the artificial lighting each day.

On the other side, your plants may be getting too little light. If this is the case, the foliage will generally be a dark green color. Move the plants closer to the tubes, increase the number of hours the plants are exposed to the lights or increase the number of tubes.

Too much red or blue light can also impact the development of plants. Too much blue light with very little red light can stunt the growth of plants and result in dark green foliage, thick stems and fewer flowers than they would normally have.

Too much red light can elongate the stems and promote tall and spindly growth.

In the next chapter, we are going to look at how you can take houseplant parenting to the next level.

CHAPTER 10

TAKING IT TO THE NEXT LEVEL

Maybe you started this book with some basic aims, like "I don't want to kill my plants" or "I want to keep my plants alive more than a month after I get them from the shop." Maybe you wanted to know how to keep five or six easy houseplants in your apartment to make it look good and give you your own small piece of nature, bringing the great outdoors inside.

Whatever your aims, if you've achieved them, that's great. For some of us, that's all we want. It works for me, for instance. But you may feel there's still unexplored territory waiting ahead and you want to take things up a level and collect cacti, or create a closed terrarium. Maybe you just want another challenge!

You've become a good houseplant parent. Now, you could become a confident, knowledgeable enthusiast. You might even help other people get started. But remember, as botanist Luther Burbank* said, "The secret of improved plant breeding, apart from scientific knowledge, is love." Whatever advanced area you might want to take on, do it from love – not because you think you have to.

*Have you ever grown the Burbank Russet Potato? He was *that* Mr Burbank. And the Burbank potato was only one of many varieties of plant he created.

 ## THE SUCCULENT AND CACTUS SPECIALISM

Most houseplant parents have one or two succulents and a cactus somewhere among their plants. But it takes a special kind of person to collect hundreds (or even thousands) of different Lithops (living stones), as Hilde and Frikkie Mouton have done in Alta Kalkoefen, Namibia – or to create a rooftop cactus garden with 2,500 different varieties, as Jaipur resident KK Agrawal has done. Maybe you're that special kind of person!

CACTUS

Cacti are actually a great choice if you live in a centrally heated home that has dry air. That's not necessarily the kind of place orchids or ferns will be happy, but cacti will love it. Like other succulents, cacti grow in arid areas and keep water inside their thick fleshy bodies. They're often spherical or barrel-shaped, a form which has the least surface area for the plant's size (meaning less water can evaporate). And they're prickly – though some have woolly spines, others have wicked spikes.

Cacti need very little water, but they do need lots of light. Putting them in a bright window helps, but you might put your collection on a table and give them artificial light for about 16 hours a day. They might also welcome a little extra lighting in winter, if your daylight hours are short.

They need very well-draining potting mix – add sand or gravel, so that the soil drains very quickly (if, when you squeeze the growing medium, it stays together in your hand, there's not enough sand in it. Add some more).

Only water cacti during the growing season, and only once the soil has thoroughly dried out since last watering. Though they don't need much water, make sure they are watered thoroughly each time - don't just sprinkle a little water on, give them a proper deluge, then drain the pot before putting it back in its saucer. That will help develop a good deep root system.

Most cacti grow fairly slowly. They only need fertilizing once or twice a year, in late spring and in summer, when they're growing. There are a few fast growing species though, like the Blue Myrtle cactus (myrtillocactus geometrizans). Give a cactus a fertilizer that has more phosphorous than nitrogen, diluted with two parts water to each part of fertilizer.

Other succulents need two or three feeds a year; they're not always as light thirsty as cacti, but still need six hours of bright sun daily. Most prefer indirect sun, as they'll scorch in direct sunlight (unless you have UV treated glass). It's a good idea to rotate them to get the sun from all sides.

For both succulents and cacti, add perlite, pumice or sand to the potting mix to ensure it drains well, and avoid getting the plant wet when you water it; either water the soil, or put the pot in water to soak it up from the bottom.

A shallow dish garden is an elegant way to display your succulents, but choose plants with the same growth rate and similar water requirements. A cactus won't be happy with a jade plant, for instance. Put coarse gravel at the bottom of the dish to provide drainage, and since there's no drainage hole, be very careful not to over-water.

SUMMARY — CARE INSTRUCTIONS FOR CACTI

- Give them lots of light.
- Only water during the growing season and once the soil has dried out.
- Water thoroughly each time.
- Fertilize twice per year – in late spring and summer (more phosphorous than nitrogen, diluted with two parts water to each part fertilizer).
- Add perlite, pumice or sand to the potting mix.
- Place next to plants with similar growth rates.

THE ORCHID EXTRAVAGANZA

Orchids, like cacti, have special requirements. In fact, they're practically the opposite of cacti: they want a humid atmosphere. They prefer potting mix that has plenty of bark in it. The appeal of an orchid is very different from that of a cactus: cacti are fascinating architectural plants with infrequent flowers, while the whole interest of growing orchids is the presence of their huge and elegant blooms.

Orchids need relatively bright but indirect light; they will do well in a west facing window, except for Vanda orchids which need full sun. They'll need misting or standing on a pebble dish for humidity; if you're really serious about orchids, you're going to be investing in humidifiers pretty soon. Or if your bathroom has good natural light, you can grow them there.

The best place to start is probably with moth orchids (phalaenopsis). These need a specialist orchid compost, and they also need a clear glass or plastic container. This is because their roots, most unusually, photosynthesize just like their leaves, and need access to light. You'll see the roots twist and turn around the pot – orchids are the only houseplant that actually seems to like being root-bound.

Even though they love humidity, orchids don't like too much watering; wait til the pot has dried out (feels light) and with phalaenopsis, wait til the roots are silvery white before you give them another watering. Tepid water is ideal. During the growing season, give them some orchid fertilizer.

Many people are bought a moth orchid which has a single bunch of flowers, and it never flowers again. That's because they don't know the secret of encouraging new flowers. Once the first flowers have fallen, cut off the flowering stem just above a node. A new stem should then appear, and this will bear the flowers. Other orchids always flower on a new stem, so cut the old stem right down to the ground and wait for a new one to grow.

There's a different trick with cymbidium orchids; you need to drop the night temperatures as you move from midsummer into late summer in order for them to get flowering.

The most common pests are mealybugs, sooty mold, and scale. Using a soapy sponge to clean the leaves every so often can help prevent these pests.

One of the great joys of orchids is the sheer number of different varieties. Even phalaenopsis has seventy-five different species; you could also try spathoglottis orchids, mostly from India and Southeast Asia, which are also an easy introduction to the orchid world.

Other species which do not present particular difficulties are:

- Psychopsis 'butterfly' orchids with their speckled foliage.
- Cattleya, with different colors of freckled and streaky flower.
- Cymbidium 'boat' orchids with multiple, brightly colored flower spikes.
- Ludisia, with tiny white flowers.

If you become a really good orchid parent, then you can try more difficult varieties such as Vanda orchids, Vanilla orchid, and Schomburgkia or Rhynchostylis orchids.

Best news of all, even though some orchids can be expensive to buy, they can all be divided to propagate.

SUMMARY — CARE INSTRUCTIONS FOR ORCHIDS

- Place near bright but indirect light.
- Mist or stand on a pebble dish for humidity.
- Watering – wait until the pot has dried out. Use tepid water.
- Fertilize with orchid food during growing season.
- Get rid of pests with a soapy sponge.

PHALAENOPSIS

 ## CREATING A TERRARIUM

Creating a terrarium is a different kind of challenge for the houseplant grower. A terrarium can be a completely closed ecosystem or open to the air – a 'garden in a bottle' or a garden in a fish bowl, so to speak.

A closed terrarium is basically its own little planet, and could survive indefinitely without your intervention; it recycles water vapor and nutrients since there is no way for the water to evaporate. One terrarium has been living since 1960!

Terrariums are low-maintenance, fascinating, beautiful, and a great way of creating a miniature indoor jungle if you have relatively little space. The art lies in the initial design.

HOW TO MAKE A TERRARIUM

For a closed terrarium, you'll need a sealed container. Bottles and demijohns are classic choices, though you'll have to plant them with chopsticks through the narrow neck; easier to plant are fish bowls, candy jars, and even glass French press cafetieres. Whatever container you pick, the ecosystem needs to be large enough to support itself; a Coca-Cola bottle would be on the small side but a one gallon mason jar would do fine.

For an open terrarium, you could use any glass or clear plastic container. An old fish tank could be used to create a miniature universe for your cacti and succulents; you could add rocks that are reminiscent of the desert landscapes where they live. You could recycle a large glass jar or if you have a sweet tooth, use your Nutella jars as mini-terrariums with a small cactus in each!

Terrariums don't have drainage holes, so first of all you need to place a layer of leca or pebbles at the bottom as a drainage layer. You'll want about an inch of drainage. You might also want to add a thin layer of charcoal on top of the drainage.

For the soil, you want to use coir or a very light and fluffy houseplant growing medium. In an open terrarium you might add the soil, then put the plants in just as you would in a normal planter. With a closed terrarium, though, it can be easier to put your plants in place first, and then add the soil between their roots with a paper funnel; it saves you having to dig holes through the neck of the container. You need to get the soil pretty close to the level with the soil the plants came in, but it doesn't have to be exact.

Finally, do any landscaping you want, for instance using rocks or driftwood to create an interesting landscape. See the picture as an example for inspiration!

TERRARIUM

The choice between an open and a closed terrarium isn't just an aesthetic one; different plants prefer different kinds of terrarium. A closed terrarium will be humid, so ferns work well in one; other plants that enjoy this environment include:

- Carnivorous plants
- Air plants
- Peperomia
- Mosses
- White nerve plant
- Spiderwort
- Chinese money plant

Succulents and cacti will not grow in a closed system; it's far too wet for them. On the other hand, mosses won't live in an open container.

It's quite difficult to create a self-sustaining ecosystem. The plants mustn't grow too fast for their container; they need to be disease resistant; and they need to create enough biomass to support the life cycle. So it isn't at all a bad idea to buy a kit for your first terrarium; they are easily available and include everything you need.

A terrarium needs bright, indirect light, so north-facing windows are a great choice. Maintenance for a completely closed terrarium basically means dusting it occasionally, though you may want to open it up to do a little pruning from time to time.

Open terrariums are fine for cacti and succulents. They dry out quickly, but you can create a miniature world inside them just as you can with closed jars.

Terrariums are a really great project to carry out with kids, teaching them how natural processes work and encouraging them to be creative and get their hands dirty. They're also your best way to grow mosses and ferns, if those are the plants you love.

 ## VENTURING INTO HYDROPONICS

You can grow houseplant cuttings in water, for a while. But hydroponics offers something different, the chance to grow plants with no soil involved at any stage. It's great if you want to grow edible plants indoors, and it's what I like to call 'geek gardening,' with every single input measured and controlled.

Typically, hydroponics uses grow lights rather than natural light, and controls for the temperature and humidity, as well as the nutrients provided in the water. Gravel or sand might be used to anchor the plant's roots but there is no soil at all.

There are different ways of providing the water. Wick systems are the easiest – and the oldest, if you count the Aztecs' *chinampa* system of floating island agriculture! Then there are flood-and-drain and drip systems.

Many big salad farmers use hydroponic systems. And you can use hydroponics at home, too. Unless you spend really big bucks it won't be a system like the big guys use but the principle is the same.

The simplest DIY system has a reservoir which holds the nutrients in solution, and a growing tray which holds the plants, plus a wick to deliver the nutrients to the plants. This system doesn't even need a pump. But because a wick is slow at feeding nutrients, you can only grow smaller plants with this system, like herbs, salads, and baby spinach.

You could move up to an active system to grow tomatoes, strawberries, or bell peppers. Using a pump passes the nutrients to the plants much faster, so you're less limited in the kinds of plants you can grow.

Maintenance is fairly simple. You'll need to clean and refill the water/nutrient mix at least once a month. However, because all the inputs need to be controlled, there's a lot of measuring to do; you'll want to monitor the water's pH, the water temperature (which should stay at 65-70F, 18-21C), and the hours of light that the plants are getting. Monitoring and controlling pH levels is very important as the level needs to remain consistently between 5.8 and 6.3. You may also need to install a ventilation system, depending on the size of your tank.

A very basic hydroponics exercise which is fun to do with children is to grow hydroponic vegetables from garbage. Take some carrot tops, the bottom of a Chinese cabbage, or the ends of scallions, and use a cocktail stick or wooden kebab skewer to support them above a cup of water, with the bottom touching the water. They'll start growing again, at least for a while!

NURTURING RARE AND EXOTIC SPECIES

Rare and exotic plants have always had a special allure. In the nineteenth century, botanists scoured the world for new varieties of plant, the rarer and more difficult to grow the better. You no longer need to mount an expedition in order to find exotic species but some of the less common plants are still demanding to grow and will really challenge your growing skills.

If you follow this path you may find you end up swapping plants internationally with other expert growers. For instance, Max Sneier of The New Green specializes in exotic plants starting with… monstera? Surely there's some mistake! That's not exotic!

Well, Max grows some varieties that are quite difficult to get hold of. Monstera 'Thai Constellation,' for instance, has marvelous foliage with scatters of tiny white spots and white streaks, while Monstera 'Albo Variegata,' with its huge white patches, is highly desirable, but also expensive because of its slow growth rate and slow propagation. Some varieties aren't even produced by market growers, so your only chance of getting one is to know someone who will give you a cutting.

Rarest of all, Monstera obliqua 'Peru' is what he described as the 'Holy Grail of houseplants.' It's a beautiful golden green, with more hole than leaf – as if Salvador Dali had created his own Swiss cheese plant.

So even with a really well-known species, you can track down rarer varieties. There are some exotic philodendrons, for instance, which come in pink, or have leaves a meter long; you won't likely find them in your local garden center.

Or you might decide, say, to specialize in air plants (tillandsia) and other bromeliads. These are particularly tricky to grow successfully, and there are more than five hundred different varieties you could collect, so they give you plenty of room to develop your skills and your collection. There's something quite fascinating about plants that grow without needing to put their roots in the ground, too; and because they don't need to be in a pot, you can display them in very imaginative ways.

For instance, you could hang them on a wire frame, use hanging ceramic holders, or mount them on a piece of driftwood. Some people hang them in glass globes. Or you could put them in individual terrariums, which can help you maintain the humidity that they desire. You could put them in the bathroom or even devote an indoor 'greenhouse' to them so they have humid air without making your entire house damp.

While most air plants are greenish, there are some quite spectacular varieties. Tillandsia ionantha 'Fuego' has pinkish orange tips, and Tillandsia stricta has vivid purple blooms; T. brachycaulos has reddish fringed leaves, and T. tectorum 'Ecuador' has lovely silver fuzz. Different colors are matched by different shapes and textures; some are curly-leaved, for instance.

To keep air plants clean and healthy, you should have a once- or twice-weekly watering day. Some plants will want to be soaked for up to half an hour, while others will just require dunking for a few seconds. Once a month during the growing season (spring and summer) you should add a diluted bromeliad-specific fertilizer to the water. And of course, make sure the plants have dried off properly before you put them back on display. You can also remove any yellowing or dead leaves, to ensure they look pristine. In between waterings, you can mist your air plants with a spray, if they need it.

Propagating air plants can be done by detaching the 'pups' or plantlets which grow at the base of the plant. Once the pup has developed its own roots, you can twist it until it detaches from the parent; don't cut it off, as air plants are quite sensitive. Give it a piece of bark or driftwood and use a wire or a little dab of non-toxic adhesive to keep it in place till it gets rooted.

The sad news about air plants is that any individual plant will only live for a couple of years and will only bloom once in its life. But if you propagate them through pups, you'll never lose the family line.

Maybe I still haven't mentioned the thing that will grab you. Maybe banana plants or even pineapples are going to be your 'thing'… they probably won't produce fruit, but you can always hope! Maybe you'll take up the challenge of growing aquatic plants indoors - that's even harder than growing air plants. Or maybe you'll try to create tiny landscapes using succulents, driftwood and rocks to evoke natural forms. Watch out though, once you fall in love with a certain kind of plant, being a plant parent can become a heavy-duty addiction!

CONCLUSION

If you've read this book right the way through, that was a whole lot of information to acquire in quite a short time. You may be feeling a bit overwhelmed, so sit down and take a breath.

I hope that as well as all that information, though, you got the very clear message that growing houseplants successfully is not rocket science and doesn't demand a 'green thumb' or any other sort of special talent. Individual plants have their preferences but if you buy from good growers, read the information on the plant label, and stick to a basic routine, you'll be able to keep them in good health.

(Okay, some plants are just difficult. But you don't have to grow those ones).

Once you get the basics right, you'll be able to transform your home from bare walls to indoor jungle in short order. There are so many plants out there that are easy to grow, from really popular and well-known ones like spider plant and snake plant to amazing cacti and moth orchids.

Remember I declared myself a plant murderer? I haven't killed a plant for three years. And my house is full of plants now, most of them 'babies' that I propagated myself. Given that I believed I had a 'black thumb,' that's pretty good going – and if I can do it, anyone can!

You're just starting out with houseplants but hopefully this book has sown the seeds of your indoor garden. Your houseplant collection will fill your home with vibrant foliage and flowers but it will also give you a real sense of accomplishment. It's something you'll be able to share with family and friends; you may even end up swapping cuttings with plant buddies or heading out to the rain forest or desert to see your favorite species 'at home.'

You may just be happy to have green herbs on your windowsill and a thriving monstera sitting in the dining room. You may decide to fill your bathroom with orchids. Or you might end up becoming a cactus collector, or geeking out on automated hydroponics systems. Your journey could go anywhere you choose.

But it starts now. It's time to get your hands dirty. Go and get that first plant, an easy-going plant that will settle in and make itself at home. Find it the right place, where it gets everything it needs, and look forward to the beginning of a great new friendship. Look forward to the beginning of your green paradise!

Have faith. Have a little patience. Give your plant some TLC. But most importantly, learn to live with it – to check on it every morning, understand the signals it's sending with a drooping leaf or a little growth spurt, and appreciate its presence.

Everything you need to get started is in this book, except for the plant, the pot, the soil, and the water. You've learned what plants are easy to grow, and impossible to kill; you've also learned which plants are a bit temperamental but might be worth the struggle. You've learned how to set up a routine that fits your lifestyle and keeps your plants healthy and happy. And you've learned about watering, fertilizer, what kind of potting mix to use, and even how to use imaginative plantings and containers to make your houseplants look fabulous.

So it's up to you now.

Let me know how you get on!

Seriously, I'd be really glad to hear from you if you've used this book to get started with houseplants. Firstly because, as you'll find, people with houseplants are always talking about them to other people who also have houseplants. It's addictive! And secondly because, if you had difficulties with something that wasn't covered in this book, for instance, letting me know will let me add it to a future edition.

Good luck with your plants. I hope they bring you beauty, calm, and happiness.

Cultivate Your Passion: Share Your Thoughts on "Houseplant Care Made Easy"

Now that you've become a Houseplant expert, equipped with the knowledge to keep your indoor garden thriving, it's time to pay it forward. By sharing your honest opinion of "Houseplant Care Made Easy" on Amazon, you're not just reviewing a book – you're helping other plant lovers discover the joy of nurturing houseplants.

Your Opinion Matters

Your review will lead others to the wealth of information and passion for houseplants found within the pages of this book. By taking a moment to leave your thoughts, you're contributing to a community of indoor gardeners who help each other flourish.

How You Can Help:

1. Scan the QR code below to leave your review on Amazon.
2. Share your experiences and insights on the book.

Why Your Review Matters:

- Your words help others discover the joy of caring for houseplants.
- You pass on the torch of passion for indoor gardening to fellow enthusiasts.
- Together, we keep the spirit of houseplant care alive by sharing our knowledge.

Thank You for Your Contribution

Scan the QR code below to leave your review on Amazon (just so you know, this takes you to the review page of Amazon US, if you live in a different country, simply change the .com to the relevant country domain suffix. Or you can go to your order page to leave a review there):

Thank you for being part of this green movement and for making "Houseplant Care Made Easy" a source of inspiration for others as they embark on their houseplant journey.

Gratefully,
Nydia Needham

APPENDIX

PESTS AND DISEASE

Symptom	Possible causes	Treatment
Leaves are wrinkled, curled or deformed	Aphids	Wash them off or wipe with rubbing alcohol; spray with insecticidal soap
	Calcium deficiency	Add lime or gypsum to soil; add calcium to water
	Thrips	Insecticidal soap, neem oil
	Nitrogen deficiency	Use a nitrogen additive or fertilizer; mulch with organic matter
	Under watering	Give a good soak; water more regularly in future
	Spider mites	Dish soap, rubbing alcohol, give the plant a shower

Symptom	Possible causes	Treatment
Yellowing leaves	Over-watering	Dry out the pot and allow to dry out between waterings in future
	Nitrogen deficiency	Nitrogen-specific feed
	Sulfur deficiency	Epsom salts spray
	Whiteflies	Neem oil or insecticidal soap will deter these critters, but you may need to treat the plants weekly for a while
	If leaves are bleached out in 'arrowhead,' magnesium deficiency	Epsom salts spray
Smelly soil	Root rot or over watering	Cut out browned roots and repot in clean soil
Droopy leaves	Under-watering	Give a good soak; water more regularly in future
Browned leaves	Too much direct light	Give shade
	Potassium deficiency	Add tomato feed, seaweed, kelp, sulfate of potash
	Spider mite (if only parts are browned)	Dish soap, rubbing alcohol, give the plant a shower, soap/oil mix
	Thrips	Insecticidal soap, neem oil, soap/oil mix
	Under-watering	Give a good soak

Symptom	Possible causes	Treatment
Leaves turning reddish or purple	Potassium deficiency	Add tomato feed, seaweed, kelp, sulfate of potash
	Phosphorous deficiency	Mix bone meal or phosphate rock into the soil
Brown spots	Phosphorous deficiency	Mix bone meal or phosphate rock into the soil
	Over-watering	Dry out the pot and allow to dry out between waterings in future
	Spider mites	Use a bit of dish soap and let it sit on the plant for a while, or use rubbing alcohol. Whichever you use, rinse it off in a couple of hours and make sure the leaves dry out. Make sure the leaves dry out afterwards, and use tepid water, not cold and certainly not boiling hot
	Scale (brown bumps)	Remove scale with a soft toothbrush or cotton swab dipped in soapy water or 70% isopropyl alcohol
Streaky, mottled leaves	Mosaic virus	Plant is unlikely to be salvageable; quarantine or throw away plant *and* soil
	Thrips	Insecticidal soap, neem oil, soap/oil mix

Symptom	Possible causes	Treatment
Rotting stem	Over-watering	Dry out the pot and allow to dry out between waterings in future
	Root rot	Cut out browned roots and repot in clean soil
Small flying insects	Fungus gnats	Yellow sticky traps, spot-wash the plant with isopropyl alcohol (rubbing alcohol)
	Root rot	Cut out browned roots and repot in clean soil
New leaves are very small	Under-watering	Give a good soak
White deposits on leaves	Powdery mildew	Neem oil, fungicide, dish soap with water, baking soda
	White mold	Neem oil, fungicide, dish soap with water, baking soda
	Mealybug	Neem oil, insecticidal soap, rubbing alcohol, diatomaceous earth
	Whiteflies	Neem oil or insecticidal soap will deter these critters, but you may need to treat the plants weekly for a while
	Spider mites	Dish soap, rubbing alcohol, give the plant a shower, soap/oil mix, diatomaceous earth

Symptom	Possible causes	Treatment
Black powder on leaves	Sooty mold	Household detergent; look for pests such as mealybugs, spider mites which cause sooty mold
Gray blotches on leaves	Botrytis	Fungicide, neem oil, increase air circulation
Rusty patches	Rust	Copper spray, sulfur powder
Yellowing between veins of new leaves	Zinc deficiency	Add zinc chelates or zinc sulfate
Stunting and distortion of the growing tip that can lead to tip death, brittle foliage, and yellowing of lower leaf tips	Boron deficiency	Add borax
Dark, stunted, drooping leaves	Copper deficiency	Add copper sulphate
The leaf goes yellow but the veins stay green	Iron deficiency	Add seaweed
Similar to a zinc deficiency	Manganese deficiency	Add sulphur
Older leaves have yellow spots	Molybdenum deficiency	Add chalk or limestone
Leaf drop	Over-watering	Dry out the pot and allow to dry out between waterings in future
Mold or mushrooms growing on the soil	Over-watering	Let the soil dry out and scrape the mold off

Symptom	Possible causes	Treatment
Poor growth	Over-watering	Let the soil dry out and scrape the mold off
Gnats flying round	Over-watering	Let the soil dry out, take off the top layer of soil and replace it
Browning foliage	Over- or under-watering	Over – Let the soil dry out and scrape the mold off Under – Give a good soak
Spider mites on leaves	Under-watering	Give a good soak
Slow growth	Under-watering	Give a good soak

REFERENCES

Allaway, Z., & Bailey, F. (2019). RHS Practical Cactus and Succulent Book: How to Choose, Nurture, and Display more than 200 Cacti and Succulents. London: Dorling Kindersley.

Camillieri, L., & Kaplan, S. (2020). Plantopedia: The Definitive Guide to Houseplants. Melbourne: Smith Street Books.

Carter, H. (2020). Wild Interiors: Beautiful Plants in Beautiful Spaces. London and New York: CICO Books.

Geiger, K. (2013). Terrariums Reimagined: Mini Worlds Made in Creative Containers. Berkeley, CA: Ulysses Press.

Han, K. T. (2009). Influence of limitedly visible leafy indoor plants on the psychology, behavior, and health of students at a junior high school in Taiwan. Environment and Behavior, 41(5), 658-692.

Horwood, C. (2020). Potted History: How Houseplants Took Over Our Homes. London: Pimpernel Press.

Howey, B. (2022, October 20). When a Houseplant Obsession Becomes a Nightmare. Wired. Retrieved from https://www.wired.com/story/nightmare-houseplant-obsession-nepenthes/

Kondo, Y., & Kondo, T. (2018). Stylish Succulents: Japanese Inspired Container Gardens for Small Spaces. Rutland, VT: Tuttle Publishing.

Kuroda, K., & Eifuku, A. (2019). Container Succulents: Creative Ideas for Beginners. Rutland, VT: Tuttle Publishing.

Langton, C., Ray, R., & Raxworthy, E. (2018). Root, Nurture, Grow. London: Quadrille Publishing Ltd.

Langton, C., et al. (2018). House of Plants: Living with Succulents, Air Plants and Cacti. London: Frances Lincoln Publishers.

Loewer, P. (2016). Hydroponics for Houseplants: An Indoor Gardener's Guide to Growing Without Soil. New York: Skyhorse.

Orleans, S. (1998). The Orchid Thief. New York: Random House.

Palmer, I. (2020). Succulents and All Things Under Glass. Ryland Peters & Small.

Pillbeam, J. (2008). The Genus Echeveria. Manchester: British Cactus & Succulent Society.

Rogers, B. (2012). The Orchid Whisperer: Expert Secrets for Growing Beautiful Orchids. San Francisco: Chronicle Books.

Schulz, L., & Kapitany, A. (2005). Echeveria Cultivars. Teesdale, Victoria: Schulz Publishing.

University of Missouri Extension. (n.d.). Indoor Air Quality: The Role of Houseplants. Retrieved from https://extension.missouri.edu/publications/g6515

Bloominghaus. (n.d.). NASA Clean Air Study. Retrieved from https://bloominghaus.com/news/nasa-clean-air-study/#:~:text=How%20Many%20Houseplants%20Should%20I,is%20about%209.2%20square%20metre

HOUSEPLANT DIRECTORY

AFRICAN SPEAR PLANT (SANSEVIERIA CYLINDRICA)

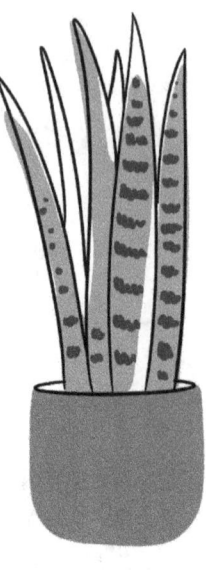

- **Temperature:** Sansevieria Cylindrica, or the African Spear Plant, thrives in temperatures between 70-90°F (21-32°C). It is highly adaptable to various temperature conditions.
- **Light Needs:** This plant is well-suited for a variety of light conditions, from bright, indirect light to lower light. It can tolerate some direct sunlight as long as it's not the hot, afternoon sun.
- **Humidity:** Sansevieria Cylindrica is highly tolerant of low humidity levels, making it suitable for various indoor environments. Can tolerate high humidity provided soil isn't saturated.
- **Care:** Easy.
- **Height and Spread:** The Sansevieria Cylindrica has upright, cylindrical leaves that can grow up to several feet in height.
- **Warnings:** Toxic to pets and humans.

Description: Sansevieria cylindrica, commonly known as the African Spear Plant or Snake Plant, is characterized by its cylindrical, upright leaves. Its modern and architectural appearance makes it a popular choice for contemporary indoor spaces.

Watering: Allow the soil to dry out between waterings. Water sparingly and avoid overwatering to prevent root rot. Sansevieria cylindrica is drought-tolerant. Water monthly in winter. Water every few weeks in growing season.

Feeding: Infrequent feeding is sufficient. Use a balanced liquid fertilizer diluted to half strength every 4-6 weeks during the growing season (spring and summer). Don't feed in winter.

Planting and Care: Robust – will survive if you forget to water or feed them. Don't typically have pest or disease problems. Plant in well-draining sandy soil; preferable a potting mix for succulents. The African Spear Plant is adaptable to various pot sizes and types. It can thrive in pots with drainage holes or even in low-light conditions. Sansevieria cylindrica is an excellent choice for those seeking a low-maintenance and resilient plant for their indoor spaces. Regularly clean the leaves to remove dust and maintain their sleek appearance. Repot every few years once roots start to grow outside of the pot and move up one size.

Pests and disease: Susceptible to aphids and mealybugs. Remove pests when you find them. Not susceptible to disease but can fungal infections from root rot. Treat with fungicides and ensure in free draining soil.

ANTHURIUM (ANTHURIUM SPP.)

- **Temperature**: Prefers temperatures between 65-80°F (18-27°C). Avoid cold drafts or sudden temperature changes.
- **Light Needs**: Enjoys bright, indirect light but can tolerate low light. Protect from direct sunlight to prevent leaf burn. Brighter light helps it to bloom. They're commonly placed near east or west-facing windows with 6-8 hours of indirect sunlight each day.
- **Humidity**: Thrives in higher humidity levels.
- **Care**: Easy.
- **Height and Spread**: Can grow up to 1-3 feet in height and spread.
- **Warnings**: Toxic if ingested. Keep away from pets and small children.

Description: Anthuriums are prized for their glossy, heart-shaped, waxy leaves and distinctive, brightly colored, long-lasting blooms known as spathes. These flowering plants come in a variety of colors, including red, pink, white, and orange, and are excellent for adding a pop of color to indoor spaces.

Watering: Keep the soil evenly moist but not waterlogged. Put pot in a tray with rocks or gravel that has water. Water when the top inch of soil feels dry. Use room temperature water and ensure proper drainage to prevent root rot. Mist the leaves regularly (avoiding the flowers) or stand the plant on a pebble-filled tray of water.

Feeding: Feed weekly with a half-strength, high-potash feed (such as tomato food) during the growing season (spring and summer) to promote healthy growth and flowering.

Planting and Care: Use well-draining rich potting mix and a pot with drainage holes. They like orchid potting mix with a few handfuls of sand and peat moss mixed in. Regularly remove spent blooms and yellowing leaves to encourage new growth and additional flowering. Anthuriums benefit from a more humid environment, so increasing humidity levels by misting the plant or placing it on a humidity tray can promote better growth and flowering. These plants are ideal for brightening up interiors with their vibrant flowers and glossy foliage. Many are climbers.

Pests and disease: Susceptible to common pests such as aphids and spider mites. If you see ants, it's a good sign you have aphids. Use neem oil. Susceptible to root rot. Ensure free-draining soil.

ARECA PALM (DYPSIS LUTESCENS)

- **Temperature**: Prefers indoor temperatures between 65-75°F (18-24°C). Avoid cold drafts and air conditioning.
- **Light Needs**: Enjoys bright, indirect light or filtered sunlight. Can tolerate some direct sunlight, particularly morning light. Too much sun can cause fading. Place near a south or west-facing window.
- **Humidity**: Thrives in higher humidity levels. Regularly mist the leaves or use a humidity tray to maintain higher humidity levels.
- **Care**: Easy.
- **Height and Spread**: Can grow up to 6-7 feet tall indoors with proper care.
- **Warnings**: Generally non-toxic to humans and pets.

Description: The Areca Palm is recognized for its graceful, feathery fronds and is a popular choice for adding a tropical and elegant look to indoor spaces.

Watering: Keep the soil consistently moist but not waterlogged. Water when the top inch of soil feels dry. Ensure proper drainage to prevent overwatering. Don't' use fluoridated water – use rainwater or distilled water.

Feeding: Fertilize lightly with a balanced liquid fertilizer every 4-6 weeks during the growing season (spring and summer) to encourage healthy growth.

Planting and Care: Use well-draining peat-based potting mix and a pot with drainage holes. The Areca Palm is an excellent choice for those looking to bring a tropical ambiance to their interior spaces, given its graceful appearance and relatively easy-care requirements. If leaf tips turn brown, give them a quick spritz or even a trip to the bathroom where it's nice and steamy.

Pests and disease: No serious issues with pests. May occasionally be infected with lethal yellowing, an insect-transmitted bacterial disease which will kill the plant. May get common pests such as aphids – treat with neem oil. Treat any fungal infections with fungicide. Can get leaf tip burn from chilled air, overwatering, underwatering, poor soil conditions or compacted roots.

ASPARAGUS FERN (ASPARAGUS DENSIFLORUS)

- **Temperature:** Asparagus Ferns thrive in temperatures between 60-75°F (15-24°C) and prefer mild, consistent conditions. Protect from extreme heat and cold.
- **Light Needs:** These ferns prefer bright, indirect light but also thrive in dappled shade. They are well-suited for well-lit indoor spaces or outdoor locations with filtered sunlight. Keep out of direct sunlight.
- **Humidity:** Asparagus Ferns appreciate higher humidity levels. Regular misting the stems or placing the plant on a humidity tray can help maintain optimal conditions.
- **Care:** Easy.
- **Height and Spread:** Asparagus Ferns typically have an arching, feathery growth habit, reaching a height of 1-4 feet with a moderate spread.
- **Warnings:** While not highly toxic, Asparagus Ferns may cause skin irritation. Keep away from pets and children.

Description: Asparagus densiflorus, commonly known as Asparagus Fern, is a popular choice for its fine, needle-like foliage that forms delicate, cascading fronds. It adds a touch of elegance and greenery to both indoor and outdoor settings.

Watering: Keep the soil consistently moist, especially during the growing season. Use room temperature water and avoid letting the soil dry out completely. Water when top inch of soil feels dry. Reduce watering during the dormant season.

Feeding: Feed with a balanced all-purpose liquid fertilizer diluted to half strength every 4-6 weeks during the growing season (spring and summer) to support healthy growth. Some may need feeding more often.

Planting and Care: Plant Asparagus Fern in loose, well-draining potting soil. Choose a container with drainage holes to ensure proper drainage. Ensure good air circulation around the plant. Trim or prune as needed to maintain the desired shape. Repot as necessary. Asparagus Ferns are versatile and can be used as hanging plants, groundcovers, or in mixed containers. Regularly clean and remove any debris to maintain their appearance.

Pests and disease: Common pests such as spider mites and aphids. Use neem oil. Common diseases are botrytis, rust, powdery mildew & southern blight. Overwatering can cause root rot.

BOSTON IVY (PARTHENOCISSUS TRICUSPIDATA)

- **Temperature**: Adaptable to various temperatures but prefers moderate climates.
- **Light Needs**: When grown indoors, place in bright, indirect light. With too much shade, the plant can grow leggy, and too much direct light can scorch its leaves so it needs a middle ground.
- **Humidity**: Tolerant of normal humidity levels.
- **Care**: Easy.
- **Height and Spread**: Can climb to over 50 feet, covering a wide area when mature.
- **Warnings**: Toxic to humans and pets.

Description: Boston Ivy is a deciduous, climbing vine known for its lush, vibrant green leaves that turn into stunning red shades in the fall. It clings to surfaces using adhesive pads at the end of its tendrils, creating a textured, green cover that transforms to beautiful autumn hues. Often grown outside, it can also be grown indoors.

Watering: Water regularly after planting to establish roots. Once established, it is quite drought-tolerant, needing only occasional watering during dry spells. But prefers moist soil where possible. Once a week during the spring and summer, and less often in winter, is typical.

Feeding: Fertilize in the spring with a balanced, slow-release fertilizer to encourage healthy growth. You can continue to water monthly in growing season but they don't need much food.

Planting and Care: Choose a container that will allow the growth you require. Plant in well-draining soil; potting mix is ideal. It's an excellent climber and will appreciate a strong support structure for optimal growth. Regular pruning is recommended to maintain shape and control its spread. Hanging baskets allow ivy tendrils to spill over the sides and give them plenty of space to grow. They are also easy enough to hang near a window for the indirect light that ivy needs.

Pests and disease: While not susceptible to pests, can attract common pests such as aphids. May be plagued with scale causing leaves to yellow. Large infestations can be treated with a spray mixture of one tablespoon of alcohol mixed with a pint of insecticidal soap. Can be affected by powdery mildew which creates a powdery residue on the leaves. Treat with sulfur spray in 2 doses, 2 weeks apart.

BLUE COLUMN CACTUS (PILOSOCEREUS PACHYCLADUS)

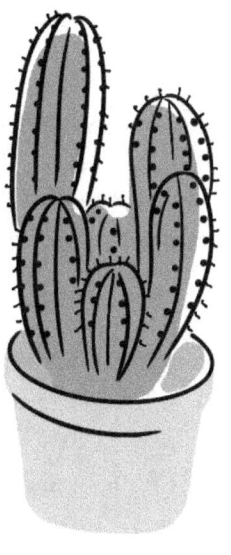

- **Temperature:** Blue Column Cactus, also known as Cereus peruvianus 'Monstrosus,' thrives in temperatures between 70-100°F (21-38°C). It prefers warm conditions and is sensitive to cold temperatures.
- **Light Needs:** This cactus enjoys full sun exposure and thrives in bright, direct sunlight. It's essential to provide it with ample light to maintain its vibrant blue-green color. The brighter the better – aim for 10-12 hours per day less than 1 foot away from the window.
- **Humidity:** Blue Column Cactus is highly tolerant of low humidity levels, making it suitable for arid indoor environments.
- **Care:** Easy.
- **Height and Spread:** The Blue Column Cactus can grow tall, reaching heights of 6 feet or more, with a columnar growth habit.
- **Warnings:** Although the Blue Column Cactus is not known to be toxic, it's advisable to handle it with care due to its spines.

Description: Blue Column Cactus, is a distinctive succulent with a unique, branching, and ribbed appearance. Its striking blue-green color adds a touch of elegance to any succulent collection.

Watering: Allow the soil to dry out completely between waterings. Water weekly in summer and sparingly during the winter months but be careful not to overwater; stick your finger into the soil about a few inches down. If the soil is dry there, it's likely time to water.

Feeding: Blue Column Cactus requires minimal feeding. Fertilize with a diluted, balanced cactus or succulent fertilizer every 4-6 weeks during the growing season (spring and summer).

Planting and Care: Plant in a well-draining pot with cactus mix or a mix of perlite, sand, limestone and organic mix. A terracotta or clay pot can help keep additional moisture away from the soil and prevent rot. Ensure the pot has drainage holes to prevent waterlogging. Blue Column Cactus is an excellent choice for succulent enthusiasts looking to add a bold and unique specimen to their collection. Handle with care to avoid contact with the sharp spines. Regularly clean the surface of the cactus to remove dust and maintain its distinctive appearance.

Pests and disease: Common household pests such as mealybugs and scales. Use neem oil. Bruises and yellow specks are common.

BUSY LIZZIE (IMPATIENS WALLERIANA)

- **Temperature:** Busy Lizzie, or Impatiens walleriana, thrives in temperatures between 60-75°F (15-24°C). It prefers moderate temperatures and is sensitive to extreme heat or cold.
- **Light Needs:** This plant prefers bright, indirect light. While it can thrive in some shade, avoid exposing it to direct sunlight for prolonged periods.
- **Humidity:** Busy Lizzie prefers higher humidity levels. Regular misting or placing a tray of water nearby can help create a more humid environment.
- **Care:** Easy.
- **Height and Spread:** Busy Lizzie can vary in size, typically reaching heights of 8 to 24 inches with a spread of 12 to 18 inches.
- **Warnings:** Non-toxic, making it safe for households with pets and children.

Description: Impatiens walleriana, commonly known as Busy Lizzie or Impatiens, is celebrated for its vibrant and prolific blooms. With flowers in various shades, including pink, purple, white, and red, Busy Lizzie brings a burst of color to gardens and indoor spaces.

Watering: Keep the soil consistently moist but not waterlogged. Water when the top inch of soil feels dry giving it at least 2 inches of water per week (maybe more in hot weather). Use room temperature water for irrigation.

Feeding: Feed with a balanced liquid fertilizer every 2-4 weeks during the growing season (spring and summer) to encourage continuous blooming.

Planting and Care: Plant in well-draining soil and ensure the container has drainage holes. Busy Lizzie is suitable for hanging baskets, containers, or garden beds. Prune spent blooms to promote new flower production. This plant is an excellent choice for those seeking a profusely flowering and easy-to-maintain addition to their garden or indoor space. Regularly remove any yellowing leaves or spent flowers to encourage ongoing blooming.

Pests and disease: Susceptible to downy mildew, viruses, fungal blights and rots likely due to wet conditions or being too close together. Can be affected by common pests such as aphids and spider mites. Treat with neem oil.

CHINESE EVERGREEN (AGLAONEMA)

- **Temperature**: Prefers average indoor temperatures between 65-80°F (18-27°C).
- **Light Needs**: Thrives in low to moderate indirect light but can tolerate brighter conditions with caution. Needs a few hours of sunlight otherwise can lose its colors, although darker varieties can grow in near-shade. The lighter the variegation on its leaves, the more sunlight it will need. Don't put in direct sunlight as it can burn their delicate leaves.
- **Humidity**: Adaptable to various humidity levels but prefers moderate to higher humidity. Doesn't like drafts.
- **Care**: Easy to moderate.
- **Height and Spread**: Varies by variety, typically reaching up to 1-3 feet tall and wide.
- **Warnings**: Toxic if ingested. Keep away from pets and small children.

Description: The Chinese Evergreen, or Aglaonema, is known for its attractive, broad, lance-shaped leaves with beautiful variegation. It's a popular houseplant due to its versatility and adaptability to different light conditions, making it a great choice for various indoor settings. Chinese Evergreens come in various shades of green, often accented with silver, gray, red, or pink tones.

Watering: Keep the soil lightly moist but not waterlogged. Water when the top inch of soil is dry, using room temperature water. Ensure proper drainage to prevent overwatering and root rot. If soil is retaining too much water, try mixing in sand or perlite to aid drainage.

Feeding: Fertilize with a balanced liquid fertilizer every 6 weeks during the growing season (spring and summer) to promote healthy growth or at the beginning and end of the growing season.

Planting and Care: Use well-draining acidic soil and a pot with good drainage. Repot as needed, usually every couple of years or when the plant becomes root-bound. They're an ideal choice for interiors with varying light levels, adding an aesthetic appeal with their vibrant foliage. Regularly wipe the leaves with a damp cloth to remove dust and allow optimal light absorption.

Pests and disease: Common household pests such as mealybugs and scales. Use neem oil. Overwatering can cause fungal diseases.

CORN PLANTS (DRACAENA FRAGRANS)

- **Temperature:** Corn Plants thrive in temperatures between 60-75°F (15-24°C) and prefer mild, consistent conditions. Protect from drafts and sudden temperature changes.
- **Light Needs:** These plants enjoy bright, indirect light but can tolerate lower light conditions, although too little light will result in color loss in the leaves. They are well-suited for well-lit indoor spaces with filtered sunlight. Protect from direct sunlight.
- **Humidity:** Corn Plants are adaptable to standard household humidity levels. No specific adjustments are necessary. Protect against drafts and heating vents. Use a humidifier or place on a tray of pebbles and water if you need to increase the humidity.
- **Care:** Easy.
- **Height and Spread:** Corn Plants typically have an upright growth habit, reaching a height of 4-6 feet indoors with a moderate spread.
- **Warnings:** While not highly toxic, Corn Plants may cause mild irritation or vomiting if ingested. Keep away from pets and children.

Description: Dracaena fragrans, commonly known as Corn Plant or Mass Cane, is recognized for its attractive, arching leaves that resemble corn stalks. It adds a touch of tropical elegance to indoor spaces.

Watering: Allow the top inch of soil to dry between waterings. Water sparingly, especially during the dormant season (winter). Use room temperature water and avoid overwatering to prevent root rot. Reducing watering in late fall and winter.

Feeding: Feed with a balanced liquid fertilizer diluted to half strength every 4-6 weeks during the growing season (spring and summer) to support healthy growth. Feed sparingly or not at all in winter.

Planting and Care: Plant Corn Plants in loose, loamy, well-draining soil mix. Choose a container with drainage holes to ensure proper drainage. Ensure good air circulation around the plant. Trim or remove any yellow or damaged leaves. Repot as necessary. Corn Plants are excellent choices for adding a touch of the tropics to indoor environments. Regularly clean the leaves to remove dust and maintain their glossy appearance.

Pests and disease: Common household pests such as mealybugs and scales. Use neem oil and dust the leaves regularly. May get leaf spot which causes brown spots on the leaves; remove affected leaves, improve air circulation and avoid overwatering.

ECHEVERIA (ECHEVERIA SPP.)

- **Temperature**: Prefers indoor temperatures between 65-75°F (18-24°C).
- **Light Needs**: Enjoys bright light. Thrives in direct sunlight for 5 to 6 hours a day but can scorch in intense sun. If you can't put it in the sun, you may need a grow light. They're ideal for south or west-facing windows. Place outside in summer in a spot where it will receive shade at the hottest part of the day.
- **Humidity**: Tolerant of normal household humidity levels. Avoid putting in overly-humid places in the home such as the bathroom.
- **Care**: Easy.
- **Height and Spread**: Varies depending on the species and growth conditions.
- **Warnings**: Generally non-toxic to humans and pets.

Description: Echeveria plants are popular for their rosette-shaped, fleshy leaves, forming beautiful arrangements and available in a variety of colors and textures.

Watering: Allow the soil to dry out between waterings. Water, then let the soil dry to avoid overwatering and potential root rot. They are highly sensitive to overwatering so always best to underwater than overwater. If in doubt, leave a few days before adding more.

Feeding: Fertilize sparingly with a balanced, diluted succulent fertilizer every 4-6 weeks during the growing season (spring and summer). Too much fertilizer or soil that is too nutrient-rich can actually harm them and result in fertilizer burn or leggy growth.

Planting and Care: Plant in a well-draining succulent or cactus mix in a pot with drainage holes. They also like sandy, mix that is low in organic components such as humus, peat moss, or coco coir. Avoid overwatering to prevent issues with root health. Echeverias are a fantastic choice for succulent enthusiasts and those looking for low-maintenance, charming plants, often forming stunning arrangements or stand-alone pieces in indoor spaces.

Pests and disease: Common household pests such as mealybugs and scales. Use neem oil. Can also get fungal knats that hover above the soil. This can kill the plant. If they get fungal disease it can wipe them out, normally caused by overwatering. Change your watering routine. Remove plant from pot, cut away dead root and clean the rest. Allow to air for 24 hours and repot in a new pot with fresh soil.

GUIANA CHESTNUT (PACHIRA AQUATICA)

- **Temperature:** Guiana Chestnut thrives in temperatures between 65-75°F (18-24°C) and prefers consistently warm conditions. Protect from drafts and sudden temperature changes.
- **Light Needs:** These plants enjoy bright, indirect light for 5 to 6 hours per day. Can tolerate direct sunlight. They are well-suited for well-lit indoor spaces. Use a fluorescent light if you can't satisfy its light needs.
- **Humidity:** Guiana Chestnut is adaptable to standard household humidity levels but prefers higher humidity. No specific adjustments are necessary. Don't place near drafts. Increase humidity by placing in tray with pebbles and water or mist regularly.
- **Care:** Easy.
- **Height and Spread:** Guiana Chestnut typically has a tree-like growth habit, reaching a height of 6-8 feet indoors with a moderate spread.
- **Warnings:** Non-toxic, making them safe for homes with pets and children.

Description: Pachira aquatica, commonly known as Guiana Chestnut or Money Tree, is a striking plant known for its braided trunk and distinctive palmate leaves. It is believed to bring good luck and prosperity.

Watering: Allow the top inch of soil to dry between waterings. Water regularly and thoroughly and ensure proper drainage to prevent waterlogging (but they are near impossible to overwater). Use room temperature water. Less frequent watering in the winter months.

Feeding: Feed with a balanced liquid fertilizer diluted to half strength every 4-6 weeks during the growing season (spring and summer) to support healthy growth. Bi-monthly in the winter months.

Planting and Care: Plant Guiana Chestnut in well-draining soil. Choose a container with drainage holes to ensure proper drainage. Ensure good air circulation around the plant. Trim or prune as needed to maintain the desired shape. Repot as necessary. Guiana Chestnut is an excellent choice for adding a touch of elegance and symbolism to indoor spaces. Regularly clean the leaves to remove dust and maintain their glossy appearance.

Pests and disease: Common household pests such as mealybugs and scales. Also whitefly and thrips. Use neem oil. Common diseases are root rot, leaf-spot disease, botrytis, powdery mildew & southern blight.

HEARTLEAF PHILODENDRON (PHILODENDRON HEDERACEUM)

- **Temperature**: Prefers indoor temperatures ranging from 65-80°F (18-27°C).
- **Light Needs**: Thrives in medium to bright, indirect light but can adapt to lower light conditions. Too much direct sunlight will scorch its leaves. It's commonly placed near north or east-facing windows.
- **Humidity**: Tolerant of normal household humidity levels but benefits from slightly higher humidity. Excess humidity can lead to fungus on the leaves.
- **Care**: Easy.
- **Height and Spread**: Vines can grow several feet long with a spread of up to 3-6 feet.
- **Warnings**: Mildly toxic if ingested. Keep away from pets and small children.

Description: The Heartleaf Philodendron, also known as Philodendron hederaceum, is a popular vining plant with heart-shaped, glossy, green leaves. It's revered for its resilience and ease of care, making it a beloved choice for various indoor settings. In addition to occasional watering and repotting once it outgrows its container, the only care needed is regularly pruning trailing stems.

Watering: Water moderately, allowing the top inch of soil to dry out between waterings. Use room temperature water and ensure proper drainage to avoid waterlogged soil, which can lead to root rot. Don't use cold water as it can harm it by shocking its root system.

Feeding: Fertilize with a balanced liquid fertilizer twice during the growing season (spring and summer) to encourage growth. Do not feed in winter.

Planting and Care: Use basic potting mix with peat-moss and a pot with drainage holes. Or combine peat moss, perlite and vermiculite. Regularly wipe the leaves to remove dust and promote optimal light absorption. Trim leggy vines or pinch back the stems to encourage bushier growth. This low-maintenance plant is excellent for hanging baskets or placed on a shelf, allowing its trailing vines to create an appealing cascade.

Pests and disease: Can be susceptible to fungus knats which can be seen on top of the soil. If you let the soil surface dry out between watering they'll often fly off. Common pests such as aphids and mealybugs can also be a problem. Treat with neem oil.

HEDERA, ENGLISH IVY (HEDERA HELIX)

- **Temperature:** English Ivy thrives in temperatures between 70-90°F (21-32°C) and prefers cool to moderate conditions. Protect from extreme heat and cold.
- **Light Needs:** These plants do well in bright, indirect light but can tolerate direct sunlight in the winter months. They are well-suited for both indoor and outdoor environments.
- **Humidity:** English Ivy is adaptable to various humidity levels. No specific adjustments are necessary.
- **Care:** Easy.
- **Height and Spread:** English Ivy has a trailing or climbing growth habit, with a spread that can be extensive.
- **Warnings:** While not highly toxic, English Ivy may cause mild irritation if ingested. Keep away from pets and children.

Description: Hedera helix, commonly known as English Ivy, is a classic and versatile plant known for its trailing or climbing vines and distinctive lobed leaves. It is a popular choice for both indoor and outdoor settings. English ivy does well planted in containers or baskets where its trailing vines can hang down.

Watering: Keep the soil consistently moist but not waterlogged. Water sparingly during the dormant season (winter). Use room temperature water and avoid overwatering to prevent root rot. Actually prefers to be on the dry side so let the soil dry out before watering again.

Feeding: Feed with a balanced liquid fertilizer diluted to half strength every 2 weeks during the growing season (spring and summer) to support healthy growth. Use 20-20-20 fertilizer or a 2-2-2- organic formula. Don't feed if very cold or hot or if leaf growing has stopped.

Planting and Care: Plant English Ivy in well-draining soil. Ensure good drainage to prevent waterlogging. Although it will grow in poor soil, it does best in loose potting mix. Provide support for climbing varieties. Trim or prune to control growth. Regularly clean and inspect for pests. Regularly clean the leaves to remove dust and maintain their vibrant appearance.

Pests and disease: Susceptible to common pests such as aphids and spider mites. Treat with neem oil. Can be affected by leaf spot and root rot, which generally means the plant will not recover. Remove the plant and treat the unaffected plants with a 10-1 mixture of water and vinegar (if leaf spot) or fungicide (if root rot).

HOYA (HOYA CARNOSA)

- **Temperature**: Prefers indoor temperatures around 60-75°F (15-24°C).
- **Light Needs**: Enjoys bright, indirect light for 2-6 hours per day. Can adapt to lower light conditions but prefer medium light conditions. They're commonly placed near east or west-facing windows.
- **Humidity**: Tolerant of normal household humidity levels but prefer high levels.
- **Care**: Easy.
- **Height and Spread**: Vines can grow up to several feet long.
- **Warnings**: Generally non-toxic but ingestion may cause mild stomach upset.

Description: Hoya, commonly known as Wax Plant or Porcelain Flower, is appreciated for its waxy, star-shaped flowers and thick, glossy, vining foliage. Hoya carnosa, in particular, is a popular variety of this plant.

Watering: Water weekly and let dry out before rewatering. Ensure the pot has good drainage to prevent overwatering.

Feeding: Fertilize lightly with a balanced liquid fertilizer every 4-6 weeks during the growing season (spring and summer) to encourage healthy growth and flowering.

Planting and Care: Use lightweight, well-draining soil and a pot with drainage holes. Avoid overwatering, as Hoyas are sensitive to root rot. Regularly dust the leaves to help the plant photosynthesize efficiently. Hoyas are excellent choices for hanging baskets or trailing down shelves, showcasing their unique, star-shaped blooms and attractive foliage.

Pests and disease: Watch out for common house pests such as aphids and scale but generally these don't cause a problem unless you have other house plants infected. Regularly inspect the leaves and treat with soap and water or neem oil if you find any.

INCH PLANT (TRADESCANTIA ZEBRINA)

- **Temperature:** Tradescantia zebrina, or Inch Plant, thrives in temperatures between 60-75°F (15-24°C). It prefers mild to warm conditions and is sensitive to cold drafts.
- **Light Needs:** This plant enjoys bright, indirect light but can tolerate lower light conditions. Although too dim light can cause the leaf markings to fade. Avoid prolonged exposure to direct sunlight, which can cause leaf burn.
- **Humidity:** Inch Plant is adaptable to standard household humidity levels. It can tolerate moderate humidity but doesn't require specific adjustments.
- **Care:** Easy.
- **Height and Spread:** Tradescantia zebrina has trailing stems that can spread up to several feet, making it an excellent choice for hanging baskets.
- **Warnings:** Inch Plant is non-toxic to humans but can be mildly toxic to pets if ingested. Keep it out of reach of curious pets.

Description: Tradescantia zebrina, commonly known as Inch Plant or Wandering Jew, is recognized for its vibrant green foliage with a purple underside. It's a fast-growing and trailing plant that adds a touch of beauty to various indoor settings.

Watering: Keep the soil consistently moist but not waterlogged. Water when the top inch of soil feels dry. Use room temperature water to avoid shocking the plant. Don't water directly into the crown as this can case rot. Don't let it become dry in winter.

Feeding: Feed with a balanced liquid fertilizer diluted to half strength every 4-6 weeks during the growing season (spring and summer) to support healthy growth.

Planting and Care: Plant in well-draining soil and choose a container with drainage holes. Inch Plant can adapt to different pot sizes. Prune as needed to control its spread. Tradescantia zebrina is an excellent choice for those seeking an attractive and adaptable trailing plant for their indoor spaces. Regularly clean the leaves to remove dust and maintain their vibrant appearance. Pinch back the vining tendrils to increase fullness.

Pests and disease: Watch for common house pests such as mealybugs and scale. Treat with neem oil. Can be susceptible to leaf spot, powdery mildew and root rot.

JADE PLANT (CRASSULA OVATA)

- **Temperature**: Thrives in average indoor temperatures between 65-75°F (18-24°C).
- **Light Needs**: Needs at least 6 hours of bright, indirect sunlight. Can tolerate some direct sun but needs protection from intense afternoon sunlight otherwise the leaves will shrivel and burn. Low light can cause it to become too leggy. South-facing windows are best.
- **Humidity**: Tolerant of low humidity levels.
- **Care**: Easy.
- **Height and Spread**: Can grow up to 2-3 feet tall and wide.
- **Warnings**: Can be toxic if ingested by humans or pets.

Description: The Jade Plant, or Crassula ovata, is a succulent with thick, glossy, oval-shaped leaves and a tree-like appearance. It's a popular houseplant known for its resilience and is often associated with luck and prosperity. This low-maintenance plant is characterized by its attractive appearance and is ideal for beginners in plant care.

Watering: Water sparingly, allowing the soil to dry out almost completely between waterings. Use room temperature water and ensure the pot has drainage holes to prevent overwatering, which can cause root rot. They are more or less dormant in winter so don't need much watering. Water more in summer and aim to keep the soil moist but not saturated.

Feeding: Needs gritty soil or cactus mix. Fertilize sparingly with a diluted liquid fertilizer every 2-4 weeks during the growing season (spring and summer) to encourage growth. Reduce feeding during the dormant winter period. Needs more feeding if in direct sunlight. Water the plant before fertilizing to prevent fertilizer burn on the roots.

Planting and Care: Use well-draining succulent-specific soil or cactus mix and a pot with drainage holes. The ideal mix would be sand, potting mix and perlite or pumice. Avoid sudden temperature changes. Jade plants are known for their longevity and are often passed down from generation to generation due to their ease of care and symbolic meaning of good fortune. Regular pruning helps maintain a compact and bushy shape.

Pests and disease: The most common pest is the mealybug, which leaves white patches on the plant. Wipe them off with a cotton ball or tissue soaked with rubbing alcohol. Do the same if you find other pests. Overwatering can cause root rot. Can be saved by trimming away rotting roots and repotting.

LUCKY BAMBOO (DRACAENA SANDERIANA)

- **Temperature:** Lucky Bamboo thrives in temperatures between 65-90°F (18-32°C) and prefers warm, consistent conditions. Protect from sudden temperature changes.
- **Light Needs:** These plants do well in bright, filtered sunlight but can tolerate lower light conditions. They are well-suited for indoor environments. Avoid direct sunlight as it can scorch the leaves. Rotate often so the light reaches the whole plant to maintain its color.
- **Humidity:** Lucky Bamboo is adaptable to standard household humidity levels. No specific adjustments are necessary. Keep away from drafts.
- **Care:** Easy.
- **Height and Spread:** Lucky Bamboo typically has a compact, upright growth habit, reaching varying heights depending on the arrangement.
- **Warnings:** Toxic to cats and dogs but not humans.

Description: Dracaena sanderiana, commonly known as Lucky Bamboo, is a popular and symbolic plant associated with good fortune and positive energy. It features slender, green stems that can be arranged in various shapes. According to Chinese tradition the number of stalks signifies something different. Eg 2 stalks signifies love and 9 stalks signifies great luck.

Watering: Keep the roots consistently moist but not waterlogged. Change the water every 2-4 weeks if grown in water. Use distilled or tap water that has been left to sit for 24 hours to allow chlorine to dissipate. Don't use tap water if you have hard water because it contains too many minerals. Bottled water is better.

Feeding: Feed with a balanced liquid fertilizer diluted to half strength every 4-6 weeks during the growing season (spring and summer) to support healthy growth. Speciality fertilizers are also available.

Planting and Care: If growing in soil, plant Lucky Bamboo in rich, well-draining soil. If growing in water, maintain the water level and cleanliness and change the water weekly and make sure it always completely covers the roots. Ensure good air circulation around the plant. Healthy Lucky Bamboo roots are red, so don't be alarmed if you can see red roots floating in a glass vase. Trim or prune as needed to maintain the desired shape. Lucky Bamboo is an excellent choice for adding a touch of symbolism and elegance to indoor spaces. Regularly clean the stems and change the water to prevent stagnation.

Pests and disease: Susceptible to all the common pests such as spider mites and green aphid. Pick them off and treat with neem oil. Can develop black roots for many reasons; cut them away and put in a new container of water. If you notice algae, clean out the container until it's squeaky clean. Algae is normally caused by light penetrating a clear container. If the stalks begin to rot it is usually beyond saving. This can be caused by overwatering or a fungus or bacteria.

PEPEROMIA PIXIE LIME (PEPEROMIA ORBA)

- **Temperature:** Prefers indoor temperatures between 65-75°F (18-24°C).
- **Light Needs:** Enjoys medium to bright, indirect light. Can tolerate lower light conditions. Direct sunlight can scorch the leaves so place in a north or east facing window.
- **Humidity:** Tolerant of normal household humidity levels. Avoid cold drafts.
- **Care:** Easy to moderate.
- **Height and Spread:** Varies among species, typically compact and low-growing.
- **Warnings:** Generally non-toxic to humans and pets.

Description: Peperomia plants are valued for their ornamental, often succulent-like leaves, coming in various shapes, textures, and colors. They're excellent choices for adding greenery to indoor spaces.

Watering: Prefers deep, infrequent watering. Allow the top inches of soil to completely dry between waterings. Peperomias are prone to root rot.

Feeding: Fertilize sparingly with a balanced liquid fertilizer every 4-6 weeks during the growing season (spring and summer) to promote healthy growth.

Planting and Care: Use a light, loose and well-draining soil and a container with drainage holes. Potting soil or coco coir combined with perlite or sand in a 2:1 ratio for a light consistency. Regularly inspect the leaves for any signs of disease, and maintain a consistent watering schedule to keep the plant healthy. Peperomias are fantastic for indoor settings, offering a variety of leaf textures and shapes while being relatively easy to care for.

Pests and disease: If leaves or stems are becoming soft, it may be a sign of root rot. Trim away affected roots and repot in fresh soil. Healthy root should be green or white and firm. Susceptible to common house pests such as mealybugs and whiteflies. Treat with neem oil.

PHILODENDRON (ARACAEA)

- **Temperature**: Thrives in average indoor temperatures between 65-80°F (18-27°C).
- **Light Needs**: Prefers bright, indirect light or dappled sunlight. Can tolerate lower light conditions but if in low light conditions for too much time, leaves can grow sparse. Avoid direct sunlight as it can cause leaves to turn yellow.
- **Humidity**: Adaptable to various humidity levels but prefers higher humidity. Mist every few days.
- **Care**: Easy.
- **Height and Spread**: Varies by variety, typically grows up to 1-4 feet tall and wide.
- **Warnings**: Mildly toxic if ingested. Keep away from pets and small children.

Description: The Philodendron is a diverse genus of plants known for its attractive foliage and versatility in indoor settings. They feature heart-shaped or elongated leaves and come in various shades of green, often with variegations. This plant is favored for its air-purifying properties and is a popular choice for homes and offices.

Watering: Water moderately, allowing the top inch of soil to dry between waterings. Use room temperature water and ensure proper drainage to prevent overwatering and root rot. Both under and overwatering can cause leaves to droop so gauge watering time by the dryness of the soil. It gives very clear indications if it wants more water so you can take corrective action.

Feeding: Fertilize with a balanced liquid fertilizer every 2-4 weeks during the growing season (spring and summer) to encourage growth. Reduce feeding during the dormant winter period.

Planting and Care: Aim to mimic its natural tropical environment by providing plenty of warmth and moisture near a sunny window. Use well-draining, loose, acidic soil and a pot with good drainage. Leaves will turn yellow if it gets too much water. Sensitive to salt so you'll need to change the soil if leaves are turning brown or yellow. Repot as needed, typically every 1-2 years or when the plant becomes root-bound. They are an excellent choice for interiors with varying light levels. Regularly wipe the leaves to remove dust and promote optimal light absorption. Pruning the plant as needed helps to manage its growth and maintain its shape. These low-maintenance plants are well-suited for various interior decor styles and are a perfect choice for those new to plant care. Likes climbing.

Pests and disease: Susceptible to fungus knats, aphids and mealybugs. Remove them and treat with neem oil. Can also get root rot from improper watering or compact soil. If caught early, plant can be saved by removing affected roots.

PONYTAIL PALM (BEAUCARNEA RECURVATA)

- **Temperature**: Prefers indoor temperatures around 65-75°F (18-24°C). Can tolerate higher temperatures.
- **Light Needs**: Enjoys bright, indirect light or full sun. It's commonly placed near east or south-facing windows.
- **Humidity**: Tolerant of average household humidity levels. Protect from cold drafts.
- **Care**: Easy.
- **Height and Spread**: Grows slowly, reaching up to 3-4 feet in height indoors.
- **Warnings**: Generally non-toxic to humans and pets.

Description: The Ponytail Palm, despite its name, is not a palm but a succulent. It features a distinctive bulbous base and long, narrow, arching leaves, resembling a ponytail, making it an eye-catching addition to interior spaces.

Watering: Water sparingly and allow the soil to dry out between waterings. Ponytail Palms store water in their bulbous base, so they're drought-tolerant and can handle occasional under-watering. Overwatering can kill it. Water monthly in winter.

Feeding: Fertilize lightly with a balanced liquid fertilizer a few times a year. Any more and its tips will go brown.

Planting and Care: A 'plant-and-forget-it' type of plant providing it has enough light and steady water when growing. Use well-draining soil and a container with drainage holes. Likes cactus/succulent potting mix. Ensure the pot is not too large, as these plants like to be root-bound. Ponytail Palms are slow growers and can live for many years, making them an excellent choice for spaces where a unique and low-maintenance plant is desired. Repot every few years.

Pests and disease: Susceptible to common house pests such as aphids and spider mites. Treat with neem oil. Not common but can be affected by leaf spot, stem rot and bacterial leaf streak which are generally caused by overwatering.

POTHOS OR DEVIL'S IVY (EPIPREMNUM AUREUM)

- **Temperature**: Prefers average indoor temperatures between 65-85°F (18-29°C).
- **Light Needs**: Thrives in indirect or filtered light but can tolerate some direct sun provided not too intense. Variegated varieties may need brighter light to maintain their coloration. Can lose leaf pattern if don't get enough light. If placed in a bathroom with low or no light, ensure they are rotated with other plants to get some light from other rooms.
- **Humidity**: Adaptable to a range of humidity levels; prefers high humidity but can tolerate low to moderate humidity.
- **Care**: Easy.
- **Height and Spread**: Varies, typically grows 6-10 feet in length.
- **Warnings**: Mildly toxic if ingested, can cause mouth and stomach irritation. Keep away from pets and small children.

Description: The Pothos, also known as Devil's Ivy, is an adaptable and popular vining plant with heart-shaped leaves that come in various shades of green, often variegated with yellow or white. It is commonly displayed as a hanging or trailing plant due to its cascading growth habit. This plant is celebrated for its ability to purify indoor air and is well-suited for beginners due to its forgiving nature.

Watering: Water moderately, allowing the top inch of soil to dry between waterings. Use room temperature tap water and ensure proper drainage to avoid waterlogging. Pothos is sensitive to overwatering, so it's best to err on the side of slightly underwatering rather than overwatering to avoid root rot. When it starts to droop, it needs water.

Feeding: Fertilize with a balanced liquid fertilizer occasionally during the growing season (spring and summer) to promote healthy growth. Avoid over-fertilization as it can cause damage to the plant.

Planting and Care: Use a well-draining potting mix that can be dry or rocky. Repot when the plant becomes root-bound, usually every 2-3 years. Choose a pot that allows for proper drainage and provides ample space for the plant's trailing nature. Regularly prune the plant to encourage bushier growth and remove any leggy or dead parts. They are great for hanging baskets or placed on shelves where their cascading vines can be displayed effectively. Grow fast – trails up to 10 feet.

Common pests: Usually pest-free but can attract mealybugs. Dab away with cotton wool soaked in neem oil. Can get root rot due to overwatering or abacterial or fungal disease. Usually pest-free but can attract mealybugs, which can be treated with neem oil.

RUBBER PLANT (FICUS ELASTICA)

- **Temperature**: Prefers average indoor temperatures between 60-75°F (16-24°C).
- **Light Needs**: Thrives in bright, indirect light for 6-8 hours per day but can tolerate soft morning sun. Avoid intense, prolonged direct sun as it can singe the leaves. If they don't get enough light they will become leggy with dull leaves. They are often placed near east or west-facing windows, and a spot with some filtered sunlight is ideal.
- **Humidity**: Tolerant of low to moderate humidity levels.
- **Care**: Easy.
- **Height and Spread**: Can grow up to 6-10 feet in height with a spread of 2-3 feet.
- **Warnings**: Mildly toxic if ingested. Keep away from pets and small children.

Description: The Rubber Plant, or Ficus elastica, is a popular indoor tree-like plant with broad, glossy, dark green leaves. This plant can be a statement piece in interior decor and adds a touch of elegance to living spaces. It's favored for its air-purifying abilities and lush foliage.

Watering: Keep the soil evenly moist during the growing season, allowing the top inch of soil to dry between waterings. They like to be kept steadily moist but not soaked. Use room temperature tap water. During the dormant season (winter), reduce watering but do not let the soil completely dry out to prevent leaf drop. Tolerant of intermittent watering if needed.

Feeding: Fertilize with a balanced liquid fertilizer every 2-4 weeks during the growing season (spring and summer) to encourage growth. Reduce or stop feeding in the dormant season.

Planting and Care: Use well-draining soil and a pot with good drainage to prevent waterlogging. Repot every 2-3 years to provide more space for the growing roots. Regularly wipe the leaves to remove dust and promote optimal light absorption. Keep the plant away from drafts, as sudden temperature fluctuations can lead to leaf drop. Prune the plant as needed to maintain its desired shape and size.

Pests and disease: Vulnerable to common house pests such as aphids and mealy bugs. Treat with neem oil. Generally not affected by disease but can get black spots from mould, bacterial infections, fungi or viral infections.

SAGO PALM (CYCAS REVOLUTA)

- **Temperature:** Prefers indoor temperatures between 65-75°F (18-24°C). Avoid sudden temperature changes.
- **Light Needs**: Enjoys bright, indirect light. Can tolerate lower light conditions but grows best in bright light. Avoid direct sunlight, which will wilt and burn the foliage. Too much shade can cause sparse leaves so choose an east or west-facing window.
- **Humidity**: Tolerant of normal household humidity levels. Protect from drafts and air conditioning.
- **Care**: Easy.
- **Height and Spread**: Can grow up to 2-3 feet tall indoors, but growth is slow.
- **Warnings**: Toxic if ingested. Keep away from pets and children.

Description: The Sago Palm, though not a true palm, resembles a small palm tree and is appreciated for its attractive, feather-like foliage. It's a sturdy and slow-growing plant that adds a touch of tropical aesthetics to interiors.

Watering: Allow the soil to dry out slightly between waterings. Water sparingly to avoid waterlogged conditions. Ensure proper drainage to prevent root rot. Has some drought tolerance but prefers some moisture in the soil. Reduce watering in winter.

Feeding: Fertilize sparingly with a balanced, slow-release fertilizer every 2-3 months during the growing season (spring and summer).

Planting and Care: Not overly picky about the soil but needs well-draining soil and a pot with drainage holes. A potting mix for cactus is ideal. Be cautious with watering, as overwatering can cause damage to the plant. The Sago Palm is an excellent choice for those looking to add a tropical touch to their indoor space, but it's crucial to note its toxicity and ensure it's placed away from pets and young children.

Pests and disease: No serious issues with pests or disease but scale and spider mites can cause a problem. Treat with neem oil. Can get root rot from overwatering or compacted soil. Can be saved if caught early by removing affected roots and treating with fungal spray before repotting.

SCHEFFLERA/UMBRELLA PLANT (SCHEFFLERA ARBORICOLA)

- **Temperature**: Prefers indoor temperatures between 60-75°F (15-24°C). Avoid sudden temperature changes.
- **Light Needs**: Enjoys bright, indirect light. Can tolerate lower light conditions. Don't place in direct sunlight because it can burn the leaves. It's commonly placed near east or south-facing windows and can be put outside in summer provided not in direct sunlight.
- **Humidity**: Tolerant of normal household humidity levels. Keep away from drafts.
- **Care**: Easy.
- **Height and Spread**: Can grow up to 4-6 feet tall indoors.
- **Warnings**: Mildly toxic if ingested. Keep away from pets and children.

Description: The Schefflera, known for its leafy, umbrella-shaped foliage, is a popular houseplant that adds a touch of greenery to interior spaces.

Watering: Keep the soil consistently moist but not waterlogged during the growing season and spray the leaves with water. Water when the top inch of soil feels dry. Ensure proper drainage to avoid overwatering. Cut back during winter and don't water in the evenings.

Feeding: Heavy feeders that benefit from extra fertilizer. Fertilize lightly with a balanced liquid fertilizer twice a week during the growing season (spring and summer) to encourage healthy growth.

Planting and Care: Use a loose, well-draining potting soil and a container with drainage holes. Regularly clean the leaves to remove dust and maintain their ability to absorb light. The Schefflera is an excellent choice for those seeking a lush, vibrant plant for their indoor spaces, offering an easy-care, decorative option.

Pests and disease: Can be affected by bacterial leaf spot and Alternaria leaf spot caused by overwatering. Can attract aphids and other common pests. Treat with neem oil.

SNAKE PLANT OR 'MOTHER-IN-LAW'S TONGUE' (SANSEVIERIA TRIFASCIATA)

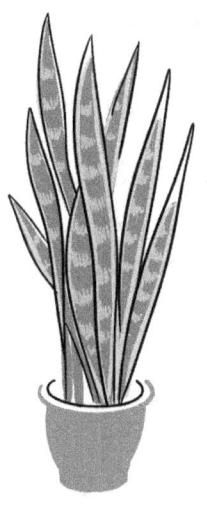

- **Temperature**: Thrives in temperatures between 70-90°F (21-32°C). Tolerant of various temperatures.
- **Light Needs**: Prefers indirect light. Avoid prolonged direct sunlight as it can burn the leaves but early morning direct sun is fine. Needs 8-10 hours of indirect sunlight. Tolerate some shade but too much can stunt growth.
- **Humidity**: Tolerant of low humidity but benefits from moderate humidity. Keep away from drafts.
- **Care**: Easy.
- **Height and Spread**: Can grow between 2-4 feet in height and spread about 1-2 feet wide.
- **Warnings**: Mildly toxic if ingested. Keep away from pets and children.

Description: The Snake Plant, scientifically known as Sansevieria trifasciata, is a hardy, upright plant with stiff, sword-shaped leaves that come in various patterns and colors, such as dark green with light green cross-banding. Its robust, vertical growth and low-maintenance requirements make it a popular choice for indoor spaces. This plant is known for its air-purifying properties and is a great choice for beginners due to its tolerance to neglect.

Watering: Allow the soil to dry out between waterings then water deeply. Use room temperature tap water, ensuring the pot has proper drainage to prevent water accumulation. Stores water in its leaves so is quite drought-tolerant and should not be overwatered, as this may lead to root rot. It also doesn't like to have its leaves wet; water by pouring in water and letting it absorb the moisture. Water monthly in winter.

Feeding: Fertilize sparingly with a balanced liquid fertilizer once in spring and once in summer to encourage growth. Too much fertilizer can cause damage, so it's best to under-fertilize rather than overdo it. Don't feed in winter.

Planting and Care: Use a loose, well-draining potting mix. Cactus potting soil is a good choice. The Snake Plant prefers to be slightly root-bound, so repotting is generally needed only every 2-5 years or when the plant becomes too crowded. Choose a pot that is slightly larger than the root ball to provide ample space for growth. Ensure the pot has adequate drainage holes to avoid waterlogged soil. Regularly wipe the leaves to prevent dust build-up and allow optimal absorption of light.

Pests and disease: Susceptible to common pests such as aphids and mealybugs. Treat with neem oil.

SPIDER PLANT (CHLOROPHYTUM COMOSUM)

- **Temperature:** Prefers average indoor temperatures between 60-75°F (16-24°C).
- **Light Needs:** Thrives in indirect or bright, filtered light but can tolerate some direct sunlight. Will also tolerate lower light conditions but may not grow as well.
- **Humidity:** Tolerant of various humidity levels but prefers slightly higher humidity. Protect from drafts.
- **Care:** Easy.
- **Height and Spread:** Typically grows 1-2 feet tall and spreads about 2-3 feet wide.
- **Warnings:** Non-toxic to humans and pets.

Description: Spider plants, scientifically known as Chlorophytum comosum, feature long, slender, arching leaves with a green and white striped or variegated pattern. They are often grown as hanging plants or placed on surfaces, adding a decorative touch to any indoor space. These plants are known for their air-purifying properties and produce small, white, star-shaped flowers, often followed by baby spider plants, or plantlets, which dangle from the mother plant on thin, wiry stems. These plantlets can be easily rooted in soil or water for propagation.

Watering: Likes moist but not soggy soil. Water the plant moderately, allowing the top inch of the soil to dry out between waterings. Use room temperature tap water and ensure the pot has drainage holes to prevent waterlogging. Spider plants are sensitive to fluoride and chlorine in water, so it's beneficial to let the water sit out overnight to dissipate these chemicals before using it for watering.

Feeding: Feed your spider plant with a balanced liquid fertilizer diluted to half strength every 2-4 weeks during the growing season (spring and summer). Fertilizing helps promote healthy foliage growth and encourages the production of plantlets but too much can cause brown leaf tips, whereas too little can cause weak growth.

Planting and Care: When potting a spider plant, opt for a well-draining potting mix that doesn't retain excess moisture, such as a mix of peat, perlite, and coarse sand. Choose a pot with drainage holes to avoid waterlogged soil. Repot the plant every couple of years or when it becomes root-bound, typically in the spring. Spider plants benefit from occasional grooming, where brown or yellowing leaves and spent flowers can be trimmed to encourage new growth. Spider plants thrive in a location with good air circulation and can tolerate a variety of light conditions, making them a versatile and low-maintenance addition to any indoor space. Easy to propagate.

Pests and disease: Generally healthy but can be susceptible from common pests such as aphids and spider mites. Look out for depreciated foliage and treat with neem oil. No common diseases.

STRING OF PEARLS (SENECIO ROWLEYANUS)

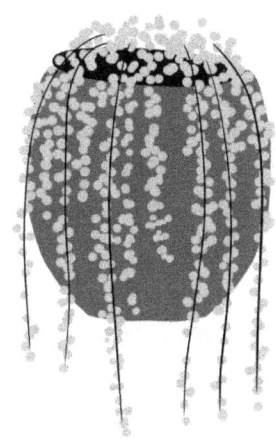

- **Temperature**: Prefers temperatures between 70-85°F (21-29°C). Can handle cooler temperatures if not prolonged.
- **Light Needs**: Enjoys bright, indirect light but can tolerate some direct sun, especially in the morning. Put in direct sunlight during the early morning sun and then moved to bright, indirect light or partial shade during the afternoon heat.
- **Humidity**: Tolerant of normal household humidity levels. Avoid places of high humidity such as the kitchen and bathroom.
- **Care**: Easy.
- **Height and Spread**: Trails or hangs, and can grow up to several feet in length.
- **Warnings**: Mildly toxic to humans and pets.

Description: The String of Pearls plant, also known as Senecio rowleyanus, is a succulent with round, bead-like leaves that resemble a string of pearls. Its unique appearance and trailing growth habit make it a distinctive and sought-after houseplant.

Watering: Keep soil lightly moist during growing season. Generally, need water every 1 to 2 weeks. Water thoroughly but be careful not to over-water. Ensure proper drainage to prevent water accumulation, as excessive moisture can lead to root rot.

Feeding: Fertilize sparingly, approximately every 2 weeks during the growing season (spring and summer), using a balanced liquid fertilizer or water-soluble fertilizer to encourage healthy growth. Feed every 6 weeks in winter.

Planting and Care: Use well-draining soil and a container with drainage holes. A good choice is cactus mix. Regularly inspect the plant for any signs of overwatering, as the pearls can be prone to rot if the soil remains too damp. Consider hanging the plant to allow the trailing stems to develop freely. This unique plant is perfect for hanging baskets or placed on elevated surfaces, allowing its distinctive bead-like leaves to cascade attractively.

Pests and disease: Susceptible to common pests such as aphids and whiteflies, which are often attracted to an unhealthy plant caused by high humidity or poor drainage. Treat with neem oil. If they get root rot, dry out and see if it recovers.

SWISS CHEESE PLANT (MONSTERA DELICIOSA)

- **Temperature**: Thrives in warm temperatures between 65-85°F (18-29°C).
- **Light Needs**: Prefers bright, indirect light. Can tolerate lower light but may slow down growth. Avoid direct sunlight in the afternoons as it can burn the foliage. Set outside once a year in direct morning sunlight for a few hours a day to encourage lush growth. They are commonly placed near east or west-facing windows.
- **Humidity**: Tolerant of normal household humidity levels but appreciates slightly higher humidity. Mist the foliage with water spray to increase humidity.
- **Care**: Easy.
- **Height and Spread**: Fast growth rate and vining habit. Vines can grow up to 3-8 feet in height and 1-3 feet wide.
- **Warnings**: Non-toxic to humans and pets.

Description: The Monstera deliciosa, also known as the Swiss Cheese Plant, is recognized by its large, perforated leaves that develop as the plant matures. It's a striking plant that adds a tropical touch to interiors. This climbing plant is popular for its unique leaf structure and makes an excellent statement piece in any indoor space.

Watering: Water moderately every 1-2 weeks in growing season, allowing the top inch of soil to dry between waterings. Use room temperature water and ensure the pot has drainage holes to prevent water accumulation. Don't add the drained water back in to the plant. Avoid overwatering as it can lead to root rot. Water infrequently in winter.

Feeding: Fertilize with a balanced nitrogen-rich liquid fertilizer every 2-4 weeks during the growing season (spring and summer) to encourage healthy growth. Reduce feeding during the dormant winter period.

Planting and Care: Use well-draining soil and a pot with good drainage. Repot every 1-2 years or when the roots become too crowded. Regularly wipe the leaves with a damp cloth to remove dust and allow optimal light absorption. Consider providing a support or trellis for climbing if desired. This plant benefits from occasional pruning to manage its growth and encourage a bushier appearance. Swiss Cheese Plants are ideal for spaces where their unique, holey leaves can make a visual impact. They are excellent choices for hanging baskets or as a trailing plant.

Pests and disease: Dusting the leaves with a damp cloth will help deter pests. Can attract mealybugs, aphids and other common pests. Treat with neem oil. If you notice browning tips, it may have contracted a fungus due to overwatering. Can be susceptible to mosaic virus.

TRADESCANTIA/SILVER INCH PLANT (TRADESCANTIA SILLAMONTANA)

- **Temperature**: Prefers indoor temperatures between 60-80°F (15-27°C). Protect from extreme temperatures.
- **Light Needs**: Enjoys bright, indirect light. Can adapt to lower light conditions but may affect the plant's appearance. It's commonly placed near east or south-facing windows
- **Humidity**: Tolerant of normal household humidity levels but prefers high levels. Mist occasionally.
- **Care**: Easy.
- **Height and Spread**: Typically grows up to 6-12 inches tall and can spread extensively.
- **Warnings**: Can be mildly toxic to humans and pets.

Description: The Silver Inch Plant is recognized for its fuzzy, silver-gray foliage and is valued for its trailing habit, making it a charming addition to hanging baskets or as ground cover in indoor gardens.

Watering: Allow the soil to partially dry between waterings. Water sparingly, as overwatering can lead to root rot in this plant. Water infrequently in winter.

Feeding: Fertilize lightly with a balanced liquid fertilizer every 4-6 weeks during the growing season (spring and summer) to encourage healthy growth.

Planting and Care: Use well-draining soil and a pot with drainage holes. The Silver Inch Plant is an excellent choice for those seeking a unique, trailing plant with striking, silver-gray leaves.

Pests and diseases: Attracts common pests such as aphids. Treat with neem oil. Generally resistant to disease but can get root rot.

YUCCA (ASPARAGACAEA)

- **Temperature**: Prefers indoor temperatures between 60-80°F (15-27°C). Can tolerate cooler temperatures but protect from frost. Used to the desert with hot temperatures in the day and cold at night.
- **Light Needs**: Enjoys bright, indirect light. Can tolerate direct sunlight provided it isn't intense afternoon sun, as it can cause white spots and crispy brown tips on the leaves. Too little light can result in thinner and slower growth. They're commonly placed near south or west-facing windows.
- **Humidity**: Tolerant of normal household humidity levels.
- **Care**: Easy.
- **Height and Spread**: Can grow up to several feet in both height and spread, depending on the species.
- **Warnings**: Mildly toxic to humans and pets if ingested.

Description: Yucca plants are known for their stiff, sword-shaped leaves clustered at the top of thick, often woody stems. They're hardy and come in various species, offering an ornamental look with minimal care.

Watering: Allow the soil to dry between waterings. Water sparingly, as Yuccas are drought-tolerant. Ensure proper drainage to avoid waterlogged conditions. Highly sensitive to overwatering. Water infrequently in winter.

Feeding: Fertilize sparingly with a balanced liquid fertilizer every 3-4 weeks during the growing season (spring and summer) to encourage healthy growth.

Planting and Care: Use loose, well-draining soil and a pot with drainage holes. Will grow in poor soil. Avoid overwatering, as Yuccas are prone to root rot if the soil remains excessively damp. Yuccas are excellent choices for adding a touch of the desert to indoor spaces, featuring their unique, architectural form and low-maintenance requirements.

Pests and disease: Generally fine but can be susceptible to aphids and mealybugs. They also attract agave plant bugs that suck the juices out of the leaves. You will see tiny brown scars on the leaves if it has this problem. Spray with insecticidal soap. It can also get fungal diseases, which appear with spreading black spots. Normally caused by overwatering. Treat with copper fungicide or neem oil.

ZZ PLANT (ZAMIOCULCAS ZAMIIFOLIA)

- **Temperature**: Thrives in average indoor temperatures between 65-75°F (18-24°C).
- **Light Needs**: Tolerates low light but prefers indirect, bright light for 6-12 hours per day. Can adapt to a variety of light conditions but can become leggy if not enough light. Avoid direct sunlight as it can scorch the leaves.
- **Humidity**: Tolerant of low humidity levels.
- **Care**: Easy.
- **Height and Spread**: Typically grows up to 2-3 feet tall and wide.
- **Warnings**: Mildly toxic if ingested. Keep away from pets and small children.

Description: The ZZ Plant, or Zamioculcas zamiifolia, is a popular choice for indoor settings due to its resilience and attractive glossy, dark green, pinnate leaves. It's known for its ability to survive in low light conditions and periods of neglect. This plant is characterized by its thick, fleshy stems and is an excellent choice for those seeking a low-maintenance green addition to their space.

Watering: Water thoroughly every few weeks. ZZ Plants are drought-tolerant and prefer to dry out slightly before being watered again. Use room temperature water and ensure the pot has drainage holes to prevent waterlogging, as overly damp soil can lead to root rot.

Feeding: Feed sparingly with a balanced liquid fertilizer every 2-3 months during the growing season (spring and summer) to encourage growth.

Planting and Care: Not fussy with the soil. Use well-draining soil and a pot with good drainage. ZZ Plants prefer to be root-bound and need infrequent repotting, typically every 2-3 years. ZZ Plants are excellent additions to interior spaces due to their air-purifying properties and resilience in various conditions. They can tolerate a degree of neglect and are a great choice for those new to plant care. Can grow very fast – watch out for it growing into the space you thought was yours! Almost impossible to kill.

Pests and disease: Virtually disease-free but keep an eye out for common pests such as aphids and mealybugs. Treat with neem oil.

AFRICAN VIOLET (SAINTPAULIA)

- **Temperature**: Prefers average indoor temperatures between 65-75°F (18-24°C).
- **Light Needs**: Enjoys bright, indirect light. Can also thrive under fluorescent lighting placed 12-15 inches above the leaves. Light green leaves are a sign of too much light while thin and dark green leaves are a sign of not enough light. They're commonly placed near east or west-facing windows.
- **Humidity**: Tolerant of normal household humidity levels but prefers high humidity. Keep away from drafts.
- **Care**: Moderate.
- **Height and Spread**: Typically grows up to 6-8 inches tall and wide.
- **Warnings**: Non-toxic to humans and pets.

Description: The African Violet, or Saintpaulia, is a popular flowering houseplant with clusters of small, delicate, colorful flowers above a rosette of velvety leaves. It's loved for its ability to bloom throughout the year and adds a splash of color to indoor settings.

Watering: Water the soil with warm water. Water from below or push the water spout into the soil to water. Don't let sit in water. Avoid getting water on the leaves to prevent spotting. Ensure the soil is kept consistently moist but not waterlogged. African Violets are sensitive to cold water, which can cause leaf damage.

Feeding: Fertilize with a balanced liquid fertilizer specifically formulated for African Violets every 2-4 weeks during the growing season (spring and summer) to promote flowering and healthy foliage growth.

Planting and Care: Use well-draining soil specifically designed for African Violets and a pot with drainage holes. Regularly remove spent blooms and yellowing leaves to encourage new growth and additional flowering. African Violets are ideal for adding a pop of color to smaller spaces and thrive in pots that snugly accommodate their root systems. Regular maintenance, such as gentle cleaning of the leaves and proper watering techniques, ensures a healthy and vibrant plant. Hard to keep happy in the long-term. Need pampering otherwise they won't flower (you could say they are divas!).

Pests and disease: Can be impacted by common pests such as mealybugs and spider mites. Treat with neem oil. Diseases include fungi such as crown rot or botrytis blight, which are normally caused by overwatering.

ALOE VERA (ALOE BARBADENSIS)

- **Temperature**: Prefers temperatures between 55-80°F (13-27°C). Can tolerate warmer temperatures but protect from extreme cold.
- **Light Needs**: Place in bright, indirect sunlight. A western or southern window is ideal. Aloes that are kept in low light often grow leggy and it can weaken their leaves. Direct sunlight can burn its tender skin but it can tolerate weaker morning direct sunlight.
- **Humidity**: Tolerant of low to moderate humidity levels.
- **Care**: Moderate.
- **Height and Spread**: Typically grows up to 1-2 feet in height and spread.
- **Warnings**: Not toxic, but can cause mild irritation if ingested. Safe for most pets but may cause stomach upset if eaten in large amounts.

Description: Aloe Vera is a succulent known for its medicinal properties and fleshy, upright leaves arranged in a rosette pattern. It's cultivated for its soothing gel, often used for treating burns, skin conditions, and as a beauty product. Aloe Vera is an attractive and easy-to-care-for plant, making it a popular choice for both its visual appeal and its practical uses.

Watering: Prefers frequent watering, allowing the soil to dry out between waterings. But don't leave dry for too long as the leaves will shrivel. Use room temperature tap water and ensure the pot has drainage holes to prevent waterlogging, which can cause root rot. Cease watering during the dormant winter period.

Feeding: Fertilize sparingly, if at all, with a diluted succulent fertilizer every 3-4 months during the growing season (spring and summer). Aloe Vera doesn't have high feeding needs.

Planting and Care: Use well-draining soil or cactus mix and a pot with drainage holes to avoid water accumulation. Actually prefers poor soil. Take care not to expose it to extreme temperatures, especially during winter, and protect it from frost. Regularly remove dead or drying leaves to encourage new growth and overall plant health. This versatile plant is suitable for both indoor and outdoor settings, making it a perfect choice for homes, offices, or gardens.

Pests and disease: May attract aloe scale or aloe mites. Use a mixture or 1 tablespoon insecticidal soap, 1 cup isopropyl alcohol, and 1 cup of water. Spray scale-infected leaves with this solution every three days for 14 days. For mites, prune the infected tissue to keep this plant, and any others around it, safe from harm. Cool temperatures and high humidity can cause aloe rust, a fungal disease that shows as yellow spots which turn brown. No treatment usually needed.

BANANA TREE (MUSA GENUS)

- **Temperature:** Banana trees thrive in warm temperatures between 75-95°F (24-35°C). They require a tropical climate and are sensitive to cold conditions.
- **Light Needs:** Banana trees prefer full sun to partial shade. They require at least 6-8 hours of sunlight daily for optimal growth, preferably full sun. Some varieties do better in partial shade so check its requirements.
- **Humidity:** Banana trees thrive in high humidity levels. Regular misting or placing the plant in a humid environment can promote healthy growth.
- **Care:** Moderate.
- **Height and Spread:** The size of banana trees varies, but they typically have a large, upright growth habit with broad leaves.
- **Warnings:** Non-toxic, making them safe for homes with pets and children.

Description: The Musa genus includes banana plants known for their large, tropical leaves and, in some cases, fruit production. While indoor banana trees may not produce fruit, they offer a lush, tropical aesthetic.

Watering: Keep the soil consistently moist but not waterlogged. Water when the top inch of soil feels dry. Use room temperature water and ensure proper drainage to prevent root rot.

Feeding: Heavy feeders. Feed with a balanced liquid fertilizer containing potassium, phosphorus, and nitrogen every 4-6 weeks during the growing season (spring and summer) to support healthy growth.

Planting and Care: Plant banana trees in well-draining soil rich in organic matter. Choose a container with drainage holes to ensure proper drainage. Provide support for the trunk as it grows. Trim dead or damaged leaves as needed. Banana trees bring a touch of the tropics indoors and require a dedicated space due to their size. Regularly clean the leaves to remove dust and maintain their vibrant appearance.

Pests and disease: You need to remain vigilant of many pests and diseases. Susceptible to aphids, black weevils, nematodes, thrips, scarring beetle. Look out for root rot, leaf spot and powdery mildew when growing indoors.

BIRD OF PARADISE (STRELITZIA)

- **Temperature:** Prefers indoor temperatures between 65-70°F (18-21°C). Can tolerate higher temperatures but avoid cold drafts.
- **Light Needs:** Enjoys bright, indirect light. It can tolerate some direct sunlight, especially morning light. Midday sun can burn the leaves of younger plants. They're commonly placed near east or west-facing windows.
- **Humidity:** Tolerant of average household humidity but benefits from slightly higher humidity levels.
- **Care:** Moderate.
- **Height and Spread:** Can grow up to 5-6 feet tall and wide indoors.
- **Warnings:** Non-toxic but avoid ingestion as it may cause mild stomach upset. Mildly toxic to pets.

Description: The Bird of Paradise is an iconic and striking tropical plant with large, banana-like leaves and vibrant, bird-shaped blooms. It's popular for its ornamental foliage and unique, long-lasting, orange and blue flowers, resembling a bird in flight.

Watering: Keep soil continually moist. In summer it will need daily watering as it loses moisture through the leaves. Use room temperature water and ensure the pot has drainage holes to prevent waterlogging. Underwatering causes yellowing leaves whereas overwatering causes brown crunchy leaves.

Feeding: Heavy feeder. Fertilize with a balanced liquid fertilizer every 1-2 weeks during the growing season (spring and summer) to encourage healthy growth and blooming.

Planting and Care: Use rich, well-draining soil and a pot with drainage holes. Regularly wipe the leaves to remove dust and promote optimal light absorption. As the plant matures, it might produce more flowers. Trim dead leaves or spent flower stems as needed. Bird of Paradise plants are excellent choices for adding a tropical, exotic feel to interiors and are often used as statement pieces due to their unique appearance and beautiful blooms.

Pests and disease: Look out for aphids, scale and whiteflies. Use neem oil. Susceptible to gray mold. Remove affected parts and allow plant to dry out.

BOSTON FERN (NEPHROLEPIS EXALTATA)

- **Temperature**: Prefers cooler temperatures between 60-75°F (15-24°C). Avoid sudden temperature fluctuations and drafts.
- **Light Needs**: Enjoys bright, indirect light but can tolerate some direct morning sun. Shade can cause it to look lackluster whereas strong direct sun can burn the fronds. They are commonly placed near east or north-facing windows.
- **Humidity**: Thrives in higher humidity levels. Regular misting or using a humidity tray can be beneficial. Boston Ferns are great choices for bathrooms or kitchens where higher humidity naturally occurs.
- **Care**: Moderate.
- **Height and Spread**: Can grow up to 1-3 feet tall and wide.
- **Warnings**: Non-toxic to humans and pets.

Description: The Boston Fern is a classic, popular houseplant known for its feathery, lush, green fronds. It's prized for its elegant, arching foliage and is a favorite choice for adding a touch of greenery to indoor spaces.

Watering: Keep the soil consistently moist but not waterlogged. Weekly watering is best in the growing season. Use room temperature water and ensure the pot has drainage holes to prevent water accumulation. Avoid letting the soil dry out completely, as it can cause the fern to wilt. In winter, water every few weeks.

Feeding: Low feeder. Fertilize with a balanced liquid fertilizer every 4-6 weeks during the growing season (spring and summer) to encourage healthy growth. No feeding necessary in winter.

Planting and Care: Use well-draining soil and a pot with drainage holes. Add perlite to the soil for increased drainage. Regularly remove old or yellowing fronds to encourage new growth and keep the plant looking fresh. If it starts shedding brown leaves, give it more water.

Pests and disease: Can get blight, which can be treated by repotting in sterile container and fresh soil. Only use fungicide if all else fails.

BROMELIADS (BROMELIACEAE FAMILY)

- **Temperature**: Typically, comfortable in temperatures between 60-80°F (15-27°C). Most need protection from cold.
- **Light Needs**: Enjoys bright, indirect light. Some varieties can handle direct sunlight for a few hours a day. Generally, varieties with soft, flexible, spineless leaves usually prefer lower light levels, while those with stiff, hard leaves prefer bright indirect light. Yellowing can mean it's getting too much light while dark green can mean too little. They're commonly placed near east or south-facing windows.
- **Humidity**: Thrives in higher humidity levels.
- **Care**: Easy to moderate, varying by species.
- **Height and Spread**: Varies significantly among species, ranging from a few inches to several feet in height and width.
- **Warnings**: Generally non-toxic to humans and pets but may cause mild stomach upset if ingested.

Description: Bromeliads are an extensive family of plants that boast a wide array of shapes, colors, and sizes. They are distinguished by their rosette-shaped foliage and unique, long-lasting, colorful flower spikes, making them a popular choice for both indoor and outdoor ornamental plants.

Watering: Water directly into the central cup (also called the 'vase') of the plant and occasionally mist the foliage. Ensure the central cup doesn't overflow and replace the water regularly to prevent stagnation, which could lead to rot. Some varieties are tolerant of drought but most need constant moisture. Water weekly in growing season and reduce during winter.

Feeding: Bromeliads are not heavy feeders. During the growing season, use a diluted liquid fertilizer . Avoid feeding mature plants in winter or when the plant begins to flower.

Planting and Care: Use well-draining soil for potted bromeliads and ensure proper drainage. Can use orchid mix, charcoal or soil-less potting mix. Regularly inspect the central cup for any water stagnation or debris accumulation. Bromeliads are excellent choices for adding unique and exotic touches to indoor and outdoor spaces, with many species featuring spectacular and long-lasting flower displays. Needs propagating, as each plant only flowers once.

Pests and disease: Susceptible to common pests such as aphids and mealybugs but are largely free of pests.

CHINESE MONEY PLANT (PILEA PEPEROMIOIDES)

- **Temperature**: Prefers indoor temperatures around 60-75°F (15-24°C). But a short period of cold exposure in winter can encourage it to bloom.
- **Light Needs**: Enjoys bright, indirect light. Can tolerate lower light conditions but will grow fewer offshoots and may become leggy. Rotate regularly to maintain symmetry and prevent it drooping on one side.
- **Humidity**: Tolerant of normal household humidity levels. Avoid overly dry conditions.
- **Care**: Moderate.
- **Height and Spread**: Grows up to 8-12 inches tall and wide.
- **Warnings**: Non-toxic to humans and pets.

Description: The Chinese Money Plant, also known as Pilea peperomioides, is recognized for its distinct coin-shaped, round leaves and is considered a symbol of good fortune. It's a popular choice for its attractive, easy-to-care-for nature.

Watering: Allow the soil to dry out between waterings and then water thoroughly, but do not let the plant sit in water to avoid root rot. The Chinese Money Plant prefers slightly drier conditions.

Feeding: Fertilize sparingly with a balanced liquid fertilizer every 4-6 weeks during the growing season (spring and summer) to encourage healthy growth.

Planting and Care: Use rich, well-draining soil and a pot with drainage holes. High quality organic potting mix with coir is best. This plant is a perfect choice for smaller spaces and tabletops, adding a unique, round foliage that is both decorative and easy to maintain. Easy to propagate.

Pests and disease: Not prone to any particular pests or disease but keep an eye out for common household pests such as mealybugs and scale. Treat with neem oil.

DRAGON TREE (DRACAENA MARGINATA)

- **Temperature:** Dragon Trees thrive in temperatures between 70-80°F (21-27°C) and are adaptable to normal indoor temperature variations. Protect from cold drafts.
- **Light Needs:** These plants prefer bright, indirect light but can tolerate lower light conditions and partial shade. However, if grown in low light they'll grow more slowly with smaller leaves and less color. Don't place in direct sun. They are well-suited for indoor environments.
- **Humidity:** Dragon Trees are adaptable to standard household humidity levels. No specific adjustments are necessary. If your house is particularly dry, mist every few days.
- **Care:** Moderate.
- **Height and Spread:** Dragon Trees typically have an upright growth habit with narrow, arching leaves. They can reach heights of 6-8 feet indoors with a moderate spread.
- **Warnings:** Only mildly toxic to humans but toxic to pets.

Description: Dracaena marginata, commonly known as the Dragon Tree, is a popular and resilient plant known for its slender, red-edged leaves. It adds a touch of elegance and drama to indoor spaces.

Watering: Allow the top inch of soil to dry between waterings. These plants are drought-tolerant so water sparingly and avoid overwatering to prevent root rot. Use room temperature water that is distilled or non-fluoridated.

Feeding: Feed with a balanced liquid fertilizer diluted to half strength every 4-6 weeks during the growing season (spring and summer) to support healthy growth. Feeding is not an essential part of its survival. Don't fertilize in winter.

Planting and Care: Plant Dragon Trees in loose, well-draining soil. Choose a container with drainage holes to ensure proper drainage and big enough for its deep roots. Trim or prune as needed to maintain the desired shape. Repot as necessary every 2-3 years. Dragon Trees are excellent choices for adding vertical interest and a touch of the exotic to indoor spaces. Regularly clean the leaves to remove dust and maintain their vibrant appearance.

Pests and disease: Fairly disease-resistant but can be susceptible to common house pests such as scale and thrips, as well as spider mite, which can occur when temperatures are warm and dry. Treat with neem oil.

MAIDENHAIR FERN (ADIANTUM GENUS)

- **Temperature**: Prefers indoor temperatures above 70°F (above 21°C).
- **Light Needs**: Used to living on the forest floor so prefers lower light conditions. Place in indirect light and avoid direct sunlight, but give enough light for it to grow. North or east-facing windows are ideal.
- **Humidity**: Thrives in higher humidity levels and needs a lot of moisture to survive. Regular misting or using a humidifier is beneficial. Keep away from cold drafts.
- **Care**: Moderate.
- **Height and Spread**: Grows up to 12-18 inches tall and wide.
- **Warnings**: Non-toxic to humans and pets.

Description: The Maidenhair Fern, belonging to the Adiantum genus, is recognized for its delicate, lacy foliage with distinctive fan-shaped leaflets. Its graceful appearance and fine-textured fronds make it a popular choice for indoor greenery.

Watering: Keep the soil consistently moist but not waterlogged. Maidenhair Ferns prefer slightly damp soil, so ensure adequate humidity and avoid letting the soil dry out completely. Don't let the roots stand in water. While it likes water, drainage is important to prevent root rot.

Feeding: Fertilize lightly with a balanced liquid fertilizer every 4-6 weeks during the growing season (spring and summer) to encourage healthy growth or skip altogether. Avoid fertilizers high in nitrogen.

Planting and Care: Use well-draining potting soil and a pot with drainage holes. Incorporate organic matter into the soil. Regularly mist the leaves or place the pot on a humidity tray to maintain higher humidity levels. Ensure the fern receives good air circulation to prevent issues like mildew. This delicate fern is a perfect choice for adding an elegant and airy touch to indoor spaces, but it requires a bit more attention due to its specific care needs.

Pests and disease: May attract scale and mealybugs. Treat with neem oil. May get root rot, leaf spot or powdery mildew but uncommon.

MOTH ORCHID (PHALAENOPSIS)

- **Temperature:** Phalaenopsis Orchids prefer temperatures between 75-85°F (23-29°C) during the day and a slight drop at night (to encourage it to bloom) but can survive in 65-70°F (18-21°C). They are sensitive to sudden temperature changes. The higher the temperature, the greater its need for humidity.
- **Light Needs:** These orchids thrive in bright, indirect light, which encourages optimal flowering. Protect them from direct sunlight, as it can scorch their leaves. They are suitable for well-lit indoor environments. In winter, place in south-facing window, in summer place in east or north-facing windows. Rotate from time-to-time for even growth. Can use fluorescent tubes if needed.
- **Humidity:** Phalaenopsis Orchids prefer higher humidity levels. Regular misting or placing the pot on a humidity tray can help create an optimal environment.
- **Care:** Moderate.
- **Height and Spread:** Phalaenopsis Orchids typically have an upright growth habit with long, arching flower spikes. The size varies depending on the specific hybrid.
- **Warnings:** Non-toxic, making them safe for homes with pets and children.

Description: Phalaenopsis Orchids, commonly known as Moth Orchids, are prized for their elegant, butterfly-like flowers. They come in a variety of colors and patterns, adding a touch of exotic beauty to indoor spaces.

Watering: Water Phalaenopsis Orchids when the bark in the pot feels dry to the touch, which will be weekly in growing season. Use room temperature or warm water over the plant, bark and roots 3 or 4 times over 10 minutes. Avoid waterlogging so ensure completely drained before returning it to window. Ensure the pot has drainage holes. Low tolerance for drought. Water every few weeks in off-season.

Feeding: Feed with a specialized orchid fertilizer diluted to half strength every 2-4 weeks during the growing season (spring and summer) to support flowering. Don't feed in winter.

Planting and Care: Plant Phalaenopsis Orchids in a well-draining orchid mix and ideally place in a clear plastic or glass container so their roots get access to light. Ensure the pot has drainage holes. Repot when the orchid outgrows its container or the media breaks down. Phalaenopsis Orchids are excellent choices for those seeking the allure of blooming orchids in their indoor spaces. Regularly clean the leaves to remove dust and maintain their vibrant appearance.

Pests and disease: Can sometimes experience fungal conditions such as leaf spot or flower blight. Remove affected part of plant and treat with fungicide. Rarely encounter pest problems. If you find any, treat with neem oil or a soapy sponge.

NERVE PLANT (FITTONIA ALBIVENIS)

- **Temperature**: Prefers indoor temperatures around 60-80°F (15-27°C).
- **Light Needs**: Enjoys medium to bright, indirect light but can tolerate lower light conditions and can even be kept in the bathroom with low lighting. May need to use fluorescent lights. It's commonly placed near east or west-facing windows.
- **Humidity**: Requires higher humidity levels. Regular misting or using a humidifier can be beneficial.
- **Care**: Moderate.
- **Height and Spread**: Typically grows up to 6-12 inches tall and can spread extensively.
- **Warnings**: Generally non-toxic to humans and pets.

Description: The Fittonia, or Nerve plant, is valued for its striking, veined foliage in vibrant colors, adding a lively touch to indoor spaces.

Watering: Can be hard to keep happy and keeping the plant appropriately moist can be a challenge. Nerve plant is prone to collapse if it's allowed to dry out. Keep the soil consistently moist but not waterlogged. Water when the top inch of soil feels dry. Ensure proper drainage to prevent overwatering and don't let it stagnate in water.

Feeding: During its growing season, feed plants weekly with a weak dose of liquid fertilizer formulated for tropical plants.

Planting and Care: Use well-draining potting soil and a pot with drainage holes. The Fittonia is an excellent choice for adding colorful, veined foliage to indoor spaces, but it requires attention to watering and humidity to thrive optimally.

Pests and disease: Can be affected by fungus knats, mealybugs or aphids. Treat with neem oil. Can get root rot, leaf spot and powdery mildew.

NORFOLK ISLAND PINE (ARAUCARIA HETEROPHYLLA)

- **Temperature**: Prefers indoor temperatures around 60-70°F (15-21°C). Avoid sudden temperature fluctuations.
- **Light Needs**: Prefers full sun where possible. But can handle long periods in dimmer conditions. It's commonly placed near east or south-facing windows. Can be placed outside in summer in a sunny spot.
- **Humidity**: Appreciates higher humidity levels. Mist regularly to show it some love.
- **Care**: Moderate.
- **Height and Spread**: Can grow up to 5-8 feet tall indoors.
- **Warnings**: Generally non-toxic to humans and pets.

Description: The Norfolk Island Pine, though not a true pine, resembles a small Christmas tree with tiered branches of soft, needle-like foliage. It's a popular holiday plant and a favored ornamental choice for interior spaces.

Watering: Water regularly, keeping the soil slightly moist but not waterlogged. Water when the top inch of soil feels dry. Ensure proper drainage to prevent water accumulation.

Feeding: Fertilize lightly with a balanced liquid fertilizer every 4-6 weeks during the growing season (spring and summer) to encourage healthy growth.

Planting and Care: Use well-draining rich soil and a pot with drainage holes. Regularly rotate the plant to ensure even growth. The Norfolk Island Pine is a charming plant for adding a touch of the holiday season indoors or for those seeking a decorative, tree-like houseplant throughout the year.

Pests and disease: Vulnerable to common pests such as aphids and scale. Treat with neem oil. Can develop fungal diseases if overwatered, which can cause the plant to die.

PARLOR PALM (CHAMAEDOREA ELEGANS)

- **Temperature**: Thrives in indoor temperatures ranging from 60-75°F (16-24°C).
- **Light Needs**: Prefers bright filtered sunlight but can tolerate lower light conditions. Avoid direct sunlight. Do well in north or east-facing windows.
- **Humidity**: Tolerant of average household humidity levels but benefits from higher humidity. Keep away from drafts.
- **Care**: Moderate.
- **Height and Spread**: Typically grows up to 2-6 feet in height and 2-3 feet wide.
- **Warnings**: Non-toxic to humans and pets.

Description: The Parlor Palm is a classic, low-maintenance, and elegant houseplant. Known for its delicate, feathery fronds and compact size, it's a popular choice for indoor decoration, especially in smaller spaces.

Watering: Keep the soil consistently lightly moist but not waterlogged. Water when the top inch of soil feels dry. Use room temperature water and ensure proper drainage to prevent water accumulation.

Feeding: Feed with a weak liquid fertilizer once or twice during the growing season and not at all during the winter.

Planting and Care: Use well-draining soil and a pot with drainage holes. Ensure the soil does not become spongy. Clean the leaves to remove dust and promote optimal light absorption. Trim brown tips or yellowing leaves as needed to maintain the plant's appearance. The Parlor Palm is an excellent option for creating a lush and tropical ambiance in your home or office due to its elegant appearance but needs perfect conditions to thrive.

Pests and disease: Vulnerable to common pests such as aphids and whitefly. Treat with neem oil. Can get fungal disease from overwatering.

PEACE LILY (SPATHIPHYLLUM)

- **Temperature**: Prefers average indoor temperatures between 65-80°F (18-27°C). Keep away from drafty areas and avoid sudden temperature fluctuations.
- **Light Needs**: Thrives in indirect or filtered light. Medium light is better for it to flower. Avoid direct sunlight. East-facing window is perfect.
- **Humidity**: Prefers higher humidity levels but can adapt to lower humidity. Needs occasional misting with distilled water or place it on a humidity tray to increase humidity levels, especially in drier environments.
- **Care**: Moderate.
- **Height and Spread**: Can grow up to 1-4 feet in height and spread about 1-3 feet wide.
- **Warnings**: Mildly toxic if ingested. Keep away from pets and small children.

Description: The Peace Lily, scientifically known as Spathiphyllum, is known for its elegant, dark green leaves and white, spoon-shaped flowers that rise above the foliage. It's a popular choice for indoor spaces due to its air-purifying qualities and visually appealing appearance. The plant has a tropical appearance and is often used in homes or offices to bring a touch of nature to interiors.

Watering: Keep the soil slightly moist but not soggy. Water when the top inch of the soil feels dry. Use room temperature water and ensure proper drainage to prevent overwatering, as this can cause root rot. Wilted leaves can indicate both overwatering or underwatering. Use distilled or filtered water if your tap water is chlorinated.

Feeding: Fertilize with a balanced liquid fertilizer with extra nitrogen (add Epsom salts) once a month during the growing season (spring and summer) to encourage flowering and healthy growth.

Planting and Care: Use loose, rich, well-draining soil and a pot with good drainage holes. Likes lots of organic material. Repot when the plant becomes rootbound, typically every 1-2 years. They're a great addition to interiors where they can add a tropical touch to the decor. If the plant doesn't flower, it might indicate that it needs a bit more light.

Pests and disease: Free of most diseases and pests. But can attract scale and mealybugs that can be treated with neem oil. Can be susceptible to mosaic virus.

WEEPING FIG (FICUS BENJAMINA)

- **Temperature**: Prefers indoor temperatures between 65-75°F (18-24°C) at night and 75-85°F (25-29°C) in the day. Avoid sudden temperature fluctuations.
- **Light Needs**: Enjoys bright, indirect light. Can even tolerate some morning sun. Find a good bright spot for it and leave it there (does not like to be moved).
- **Humidity**: Tolerant of normal household humidity levels, but appreciates higher humidity. Consider using a humidifier.
- **Care**: Moderate.
- **Height and Spread**: Can grow up to 6-8 feet tall indoors with proper care.
- **Warnings**: Mildly toxic to humans and animals.

Description: The Weeping Fig, or Ficus benjamina, is a popular indoor tree known for its glossy, evergreen foliage and graceful, drooping branches. It's a common choice for adding a touch of elegance to interior spaces.

Watering: Keep the soil consistently moist but not waterlogged. Water when the top inch of soil feels dry. Ensure proper drainage to prevent water accumulation, as overwatering can lead to leaf drop. Ensure watering schedule is consistent.

Feeding: Heavy feeders so fertilize with a balanced liquid fertilizer every month during the growing season (spring and summer) to promote healthy growth.

Planting and Care: Use well-draining soil and a pot with drainage holes. Doesn't need a lot of nutrient-rich soil. Regularly dust the leaves to remove dust and improve light absorption. Prune occasionally to maintain the desired shape. The Weeping Fig is ideal for larger interior spaces where its graceful, weeping branches and glossy foliage can make a dramatic statement. However, it might require a bit more attention due to its sensitivity to changes in environment and care.

Pests and disease: Can attract common pests such as aphids and mealybugs. Treat with neem oil. Can get root rot, leaf spot and powdery mildew.

BIRD'S NEST FERN (ASPLENIUM NIDUS)

- **Temperature:** Bird's Nest Ferns prefer temperatures between 60-75°F (16-24°C). They are sensitive to cold drafts and should be protected from temperatures below 50°F (10°C).
- **Light Needs:** These ferns thrive in filtered sunlight to partial shade. They can tolerate lower light conditions but should be shielded from direct sunlight other than morning sun. North or east-facing windows are ideal.
- **Humidity:** Bird's Nest Ferns prefer higher humidity levels. Regular misting or placing the pot on a humidity tray can create an optimal environment.
- **Care:** Challenging.
- **Height and Spread:** Bird's Nest Ferns typically have a rosette growth habit, and their size can vary, reaching up to 2-3 feet in diameter.
- **Warnings:** Non-toxic, making them safe for homes with pets and children.

Description: Asplenium nidus, commonly known as Bird's Nest Fern, is a tropical fern prized for its arching, glossy fronds that resemble a bird's nest. It adds a touch of lush greenery to indoor spaces.

Watering: Keep the soil consistently moist but not waterlogged. Water when the top inch of soil feels slightly dry. Use room temperature water and ensure proper drainage. Avoid watering the center of the plant as this can lead to mold growth and rot. Don't wet the fronds.

Feeding: Feed with a balanced liquid fertilizer diluted to half strength every 4-6 weeks during the growing season (spring and summer) to support healthy growth. Apply to soil and not the fronds as it can burn the foliage. Stop feeding in fall and resume in spring.

Planting and Care: Plant Bird's Nest Ferns in loose, well-draining, peat-based soil. Ensure the pot has drainage holes. Trim or remove dead fronds as needed. Bird's Nest Ferns are excellent choices for those seeking a tropical fern for their indoor spaces. Regularly clean the fronds to remove dust and maintain their vibrant appearance.

Pests and disease: No serious pest or disease problems but can be affected by common pests such as scale. Treat with neem oil.

FIDDLE LEAF FIG (FICUS LYRATA)

- **Temperature**: Prefers warm indoor temperatures between 65-75°F (18-24°C). Avoid drafts and sudden temperature changes. Don't let temperature drop below 55°F (12°C) at night.
- **Light Needs**: Thrives in bright, indirect light but can adapt to moderate light conditions. Avoid direct sun exposure. An east-facing window is ideal or a few feet away from a west or south-facing window.
- **Humidity**: Enjoys higher humidity but can adapt to normal household humidity levels. Use a pebble tray filled with water for higher humidity. Keep away from drafts.
- **Care**: Challenging.
- **Height and Spread**: Can grow up to 6-10 feet tall and about 2-3 feet wide.
- **Warnings**: Toxic to humans and pets.

Description: The Fiddle Leaf Fig, or Ficus lyrata, is a popular ornamental tree-like plant with large, violin-shaped, glossy leaves. It's sought after for its striking appearance and makes a dramatic statement in any room. This plant is known for its air-purifying properties but can be more demanding in care compared to some other houseplants.

Watering: Fussy. Water moderately, allowing the top inch of soil to dry out between waterings. Use room temperature water and ensure the pot has drainage holes to prevent waterlogging, as overly damp soil can lead to root rot. Ensure the excess water has drained after watering. Better to underwater than overwater. Water with the same amount when needed. If the plant is less than 2 feet tall, use 1 cup of water, 2-3 tall use 2 cups and those 3-6 feet tall use 3 cups.

Feeding: Fertilize with a high nitrogen liquid fertilizer every 4-6 weeks during the growing season (spring and summer) to encourage growth. Reduce feeding during the dormant winter period.

Planting and Care: Use loose well-draining soil and a pot with good drainage. Not too fussy but likes a soil rich in organic matter; a mix of potting soil, perlite and orchid bark is ideal. Maintain a consistent environment as they're sensitive to fluctuations in light and temperature. Wipe the leaves occasionally to remove dust and maintain their glossy appearance. Regular pruning and occasional rotation to ensure even growth are recommended. Fiddle Leaf Figs are admired for their lush foliage and are an ideal choice for creating a focal point in interior spaces with their stunning foliage. Propagating the plant from stem cuttings is really, really simple.

Pests and disease: Keep an eye out for sap-sucking pests such as mealybugs and scale. Also fungus knats and thrips. Susceptible to root rot and fungal leaf spot.

ORCHIDS (ORCHIDACEAE)

- **Temperature**: Most prefer indoor temperatures between 60-80°F (15-27°C), varying by species.
- **Light Needs**: Generally requires bright, indirect light to bloom. Avoid direct sunlight, especially during midday as it can burn them. South or east-facing windows with indirect light are ideal.
- **Humidity**: Prefers higher humidity levels, approximately 40-60%. Keep away from drafts.
- **Care**: Moderate to challenging, depending on the species.
- **Height and Spread**: Varies widely among different species.
- **Warnings**: Most orchids are non-toxic to humans and pets.

Description: Orchids are known for their elegant and colorful blooms, coming in a vast array of shapes, sizes, and colors. They're one of the largest families of flowering plants, offering stunning flowers and diverse foliage.

Watering: Orchids often prefer a drying-out period between waterings. Water when the potting medium feels almost dry, usually twice a week in summer. Avoid overwatering, as this can cause root rot. You can also check the roots; if green and plump it doesn't need water, if shrivelled and gray, it needs water. Water weekly in winter.

Feeding: Fertilize with a balanced orchid fertilizer at quarter strength every 2 weeks during the growing season (spring and summer) for most orchids. Adjust based on the specific needs of your orchid species. Don't feed in winter.

Planting and Care: Use a well-draining orchid potting mix and a pot with ample drainage. Popular mixes include bark, sphagnum moss or perlite. Orchids can be somewhat challenging to care for due to their specific needs regarding light, humidity, and watering. However, they're incredibly rewarding due to their stunning flowers and can thrive under proper care.

Given the diverse nature of orchids and their specific needs, it's recommended to identify the particular species you have to provide more detailed care instructions for that specific type of orchid.

Pests and disease: No major pest problems. But can attract common house pests such as aphids and spider mites. Treat with neem oil or a soapy sponge. Can be affected by fungal disease such as leaf algae, petal blight and phytophthora.

STAGHORN FERN (PLATYCERIUM)

- **Temperature:** Prefers indoor temperatures between 60-80°F (15-27°C).
- **Light Needs:** Enjoys bright, indirect light or dappled shade. If kept warm enough with enough humidity can tolerate more sunlight. Avoid direct sunlight, which can burn fronds.
- **Humidity:** Thrives in high humidity levels. Bathrooms and kitchens are ideal. May need a humidifier or to mist the plant.
- **Care:** Challenging.
- **Height and Spread:** Can vary significantly, depending on species and environment.
- **Warnings:** Generally non-toxic to humans and pets.

Description: The Staghorn Fern is named for its bifurcated fronds, resembling stag antlers. It's an epiphytic plant that attaches itself to trees or grows in a basket, typically appreciated for its unique growth habits.

Watering: Needs constant moisture. Water thoroughly, allowing the roots and basal fronds to absorb moisture, then let it dry out slightly before the next watering. Avoid water accumulation to prevent root rot. Should need weekly watering in summer and every 2 to 3 weeks in winter.

Feeding: Apply a diluted, balanced liquid fertilizer monthly during the growing season (spring and summer) to support healthy growth. Feed every other month in winter.

Planting and Care: Plant in a coarse, well-draining and moist medium such as orchid bark or a specialized fern mix. Once mature, mount the fern on a plaque or in a basket, allowing for its unique epiphytic nature. It's an extraordinary choice for those seeking a distinctive, eye-catching plant that can be mounted or displayed as a focal point in an indoor space.

Pests and disease: Mainly pest-free but can attract spider mites, aphids or mealy bugs. Treat with neem oil. If you see black spots it may have too much humidity.